DAUGHTERS AND MOTHERS

MOTHERS AND DAUGHTERS

Also by the author

DAUGHTERS
AND MOTHERS

MOTHERS *AND*
DAUGHTERS

SIGNE HAMMER

NYT

Quadrangle / The New York Times Book Co.

DISCLAIMER

While all of the dialogue in this book has been taken from interviews, the names and identities of the characters appearing in the
book have been altered to protect the participants.

Library of Congress Cataloging in Publication Data

Hammer, Signe.
  Daughters and mothers.

  Includes bibliographical references.
  1. Mothers and daughters. I. Title.
HQ777.H25   301.42'7   75-9211
  ISBN 0-8128-0591-1

This book is dedicated to the memory of my mother, and to Dr. Marjorie Taggart White.

CONTENTS

ACKNOWLEDGMENTS

I am indebted to a number of people who, through support, discussion, advice, or guidance helped make it possible for me to write this book.

First, to Dr. Marjorie Taggart White, without whose wise counsel and support this book would never have been written.

To the many professionals who gave their time for interviews: Joanne Turo, Coordinator of Clinical Services and Director of Treatment at Greenwich House Counseling Center, kindly arranged interviews with several members of her staff, including Marion Abruscato, social worker; Mildred Kouba, social work supervisor; and Jane Hall, clinical social worker. My thanks to all four for productive, useful discussions. Signe Lundberg, a social psychologist who has been studying single-parent families, offered useful insights into relationships between single mothers and daughters. Mildred R. Moskowitz, Director of the Borough Hall Office of the Madeline Borg Child Guidance Institute of the Jewish Board of Guardians, offered the benefit of both her personal and professional experience. Dr. Barbara Sang, a clinical psychologist and feminist, was particularly helpful in discussing the relationships between roles and other aspects of identity. Dale Bernstein, a feminist therapist and member of the New York Association of Feminist Psychotherapists, helped illuminate the question of how roles relate to identity conflicts in women today.

To my editor, Ghislaine Boulanger, who originally suggested this project to me and who has been generous with time, energy, guidance, and criticism throughout.

To my friends, who have been unfailingly supportive. Fran and David McCullough believed in the book from the beginning; Fran offered the counsel of her own insights and opened her house to me as a base from which to conduct several interviews. Jonathon and Barbara Silver have, over the years, participated in conversation and argument over theoretical issues as well as being warm and hospitable friends. Conversations and occasions with Meredith Monk, Ping Chong, and Lee Nagrin have been a strong source of support. My cousin and friend, William Clutz, taught me a great deal about disciplined work.

Finally, and most important, I am indebted to the many mothers and daughters who gave their time, their personal stories, and their insights, thus providing the substance of this book. I hope I have been true to what I learned from them.

INTRODUCTION

The relationship between mothers and daughters affects women profoundly at all stages of their lives. Not all women become mothers, but all, obviously, are daughters, and daughters have mothers. Even daughters who never become mothers must confront the issues of motherhood, because the possibility and even the probability of motherhood remains. Yet this relationship is so often taken for granted that it is all but ignored, even by mothers and daughters themselves. One woman, herself the mother of a daughter, told me she had never thought about her relationship with her own mother until she and other women began talking about their lives in a feminist consciousness-raising group. The story of fathers and sons, and of mothers and sons, has been explored and analyzed a thousand times, in plays and poems and novels, in psychoanalytic case studies and psychological research, but the story of mothers and daughters is only beginning to be told.

This book is part of that beginning. It will explore the relationship between mothers and daughters from the time before a daughter's birth, when her mother is starting to realize what motherhood means to her, to adulthood, when what has passed between a mother and daughter affects many of the choices each will make about her own life. No reader will find the whole story here; that will take many books and many years to tell. But I hope every reader will find some aspect of her own experiences reflected in the many different stories of mothers and daughters that are told here. I began work armed with psychological knowledge and an objective approach, but ultimately the voyage turned inward, as I found in the lives of other women echoes and confirmations of my own life; as I contemplated the things they told me, I relived my own relationship with my mother.

I interviewed over seventy-five mothers, daughters, and grandmothers, from the ages of four-and-a-half to eighty, before I began writing. In many cases I spoke to mothers and daughters together; some of their dialogs appear here. From the interview material came many of the ideas and insights that form the basis of the book. My interviews were with women from all classes and a variety of ethnic groups. But the emphasis is on the psychological aspects of mother–daughter relationships. Racial, ethnic, and class differences are stressed only when they seem particularly relevant because the basic psychological mechanisms in the mother–daughter relationship are common to almost all women in our society. Traditionally black women have been brought up to be more self-reliant and less dependent on men than their white sisters, but this tradition is changing as black people move into the middle class and assume its values.

The lives of women are changing. The generation of women who are now in their late twenties, thirties, and early forties is the pivot: women who have been raised in a traditional way and who must themselves begin to make changes in their own lives and the lives of their daughters. These are the women on whom this book focuses, as it explores how their relationships to themselves, to their mothers, and to their daughters are changing as they change their own lives. Mothers and daughters of all ages are living through a time of transition; as fast as the definition of some aspect of the mother–daughter relationship is arrived at, one finds that it is being affected by new forces. So the task I have set myself is to illuminate a complex relationship in a rapidly changing social context. If the focus is primarily on middle-class mothers and daughters, it is because that is where change is taking place most rapidly.

Historically there is good reason why relationships between mothers and daughters have been ignored. The conscious and unconscious ways we think about ourselves and other people are inexorably structured by social forces, which in turn have been structured by the conscious and unconscious mind. In Western cultural tradition women are regarded and portrayed largely in terms of their relationships with men. The idea of the individual self developed slowly; from the beginning, the hero and the adventurer have been masculine. As a society, we have viewed relationships from a masculine perspective; women have been considered important only in terms of their roles as the wives and mothers of men. Because society expects a mother to raise her daughter to be a wife and mother in her turn, most of what passes between a mother and daughter falls outside the acknowledged social context of men–women relationships. This has had the paradoxical effect of making the mother daughter relationship an "underground" one, whose emotional power and importance may be increased precisely because it is "underground," with no wider context than the immediately personal through which it can be channeled into a more conscious and concrete form. What is taken for granted, and therefore ignored, may be the most powerful.

If women are seen as wives and mothers, and daughters as potential wives and mothers, it is hard for mothers and daughters to see themselves or each other as separate people, as individuals. Only recently, with feminism and the work of modern ego psychology, has the idea of "self" begun to be seen as common to all people, male and female. But it is an idea that is still in its infancy. As recently as 1968, Erik Erikson suggested that "much of a young woman's identity is . . . defined in her kind of attractiveness and in the selective nature of her search for the man (or men) by whom she wishes to be sought."[1] The same idea was expressed in a different form in 1975 by a woman who, in stating her opposition to the passage of the Equal Rights Amendment in her state, said, "I don't care to be a person."[2]

Both men and women, then, still tend to think of "self," "personhood," and individual identity as masculine, whereas a woman is defined by her relationships, first with men, later with her children. Women tend to live through and in response to other people. To put it simply, they have a poor sense of the boundary between self and other, which makes it difficult to undertake activities that demand a secure sense of the existence of a separate self. The fact that such activities have been commonly denied to women has been well documented elsewhere. One of the concerns of this book is to explore some of the ways in which this weak sense of self has been passed on from mother to daughter, and to show some of the ways women are finding to change this tradition.

A mother is the first mediator of the environment for a daughter; through very subtle cues from her mother, a daughter first learns what is expected of her by her culture. She will combine these cues with her own responses and begin to form an image of herself and her relationship to the world.

A mother does not merely pass on the messages of her culture; she also passes on her responses to the messages she received from her mother. Thus, every transaction between mother and daughter is in a sense a transaction among three generations. As we shall see in the first three chapters, which explore the first five years of a daughter's life, this is where social influences are transmuted into very personal terms—where psychology and the environment meet.

The social influences on mothers and daughters have been strongly affected by rapidly changing social conditions. Before industrialization, the boundaries between home and work were less sharply defined than they are today. Women were workers as well as mothers, and their roles were broader. They had available to them a wider range of real and economically necessary activities than is available to middle-class women today. Life was difficult, but at least there was a coherent sense of expectation and opportunity extending from childhood into adulthood. Given this continuity, and the broader range of concrete activities available to women, it may have been possible to develop and sustain a positive sense of female identity, supported by the family and the community.

The sociologist Nancy Chodorow has suggested that in primitive communities, where work and home are less sharply divided than in modern middle-class Western civilization, women may have the opportunity to develop a clearer, more defined sense of self than has been possible for them in our society.[3] I am indebted to Chodorow for the expression of this idea, which I have extended to show how our own sense of women's work has changed since the pre-industrial period, and which I have used as a basis for discussing some contemporary women who have integrated both home and work into their lives, to the benefit of themselves and their daughters.

With the evolution of today's nearly absolute split between home and the world of productive work, women have been caught in a double bind that has expressed itself in the "double message" that so many women feel was passed on to them by their mothers, and that, with the rise of contemporary feminism, has been brought into the open. Quite simply, home and work are now considered to be mutually exclusive, and our society has not been in a hurry to reconcile them. Being feminine has come to mean attracting a husband and raising his children. Achievement, or engaging in producive work, is man's business. The scope of activity allowed for in the feminine role has narrowed to the point of near nonexistence, except for child care.

As the scope of women's work diminished, the idea of childhood, and of the importance of good mothering developed. And here we have another paradox: women who themselves are not allowed to assume adult roles as persons in our society—as individuals engaged in productive work and with interests of their own—are expected to socialize the new generation. As we shall see, this has presented a particular problem for daughters. A vicious cycle has developed in which women who were not encouraged to grow up raise daughters who are not encouraged to grow up either. It is not surprising that "femininity" has a pejorative ring for many women. As Clara Thompson wrote in 1942, "being a woman may mean [the] negation of her feeling of self, a denial of the chance to be an independent person."[4]

Mothering should involve both taking care of someone who is dependent and at the same time supporting that person in his or her efforts to become independent. This dual function is difficult to accomplish with sons; when a mother has a daughter, with whom she strongly identifies and whom she knows will never be encouraged by society to become independent, it is hardly surprising that she encourages her to remain dependent.

But, as we shall see, things are changing. Partly through the influence of feminism and partly as a direct response to the conditions of their lives, more and more women are finding ways to resolve the double message. They are insisting that they can work without losing their femininity, that they can be both mothers and persons, and that they can be adult women without becoming mothers. It is not easy, but many mothers today are finding ways to enable their daughters to grow up with a strong sense of themselves as persons who are women.

DAUGHTERS AND MOTHERS
MOTHERS AND DAUGHTERS

Why should it be necessary for a mother to be there like a grindstone at the heart of everything?

DORIS LESSING, *The Summer Before the Dark*

I

WHAT IS SHE TO ME?
WHAT AM I TO HER?

For any daughter, the relationship with her mother is the first relationship in her life, and may also be the most important she will ever have. As we shall see in the course of this book, the mother–daughter relationship endures as the bedrock of every other in a woman's life, including those with her father, with other men, and with her own children. In the context of her relationship with her mother a daughter first learns what it means to be a person, or finds that she is not encouraged to develop a sense of her own separate identity. Through her mother's responses to and initiatives toward her body and its needs, a daughter begins to form her own relationship to her body, laying the groundwork for her developing sense of sexual identity. And through her mother a daughter first begins to learn about the cultural expectations of feminine role behavior.

In the beginning, three main elements are present: the mother, with all her own complexities; the culture in which the mother lives and into which the daughter is born; and the daughter herself, who brings certain qualities, known and unknown, with her into the world. All of these elements interact to form the beginning of a new mother–daughter relationship. Yet, for the mother, the experience of pregnancy, birth, and motherhood also marks a new phase in her relationship with her own mother. She will bring to the relationship with her baby her own experience as a daughter, including whatever remains unresolved in her relationship with her own mother.

Dr. Grete L. Bibring, a psychiatrist at Harvard Medical School who has done considerable work with pregnant women, suggests that when a daughter becomes a mother, earlier aspects of her relationship with her own mother are revived and perhaps resolved in new ways. Earlier forms of identification may be abandoned and early conflicts resolved, until, hopefully, a daughter establishes a new identification with her mother as an equal, a friend, and a model for her own mothering behavior.[1]

The transition from daughterhood to motherhood remains the central rite of passage in the lives of women, as it has been throughout history. Until she is married and becomes a mother, a woman remains a daughter, not yet recognized as a grown woman. As one young mother remarked to me, "The only way you get off the hook is when you have children, because now you're not the child anymore, you've got a child of your own, you've given your parents a child. If you move away, and don't get married and have children, they just don't see you as grown up."

Women today are trying to change this equation of "adult woman" with "wife and mother," but it remains a powerful force in the experience of most women.

In this chapter, we will look at some of the ways in which the relationship with her mother affects a woman while she is awaiting the birth of her child, and how it first influences her relationship with her daughter. We will explore some of the ways in which cultural expectations seem to affect the new mother–daughter relationship, and also how baby daughters themselves may affect their mothers' behavior toward them. Our main focus, here and throughout the book, will be on the daughter who becomes a mother, and the ways in which her experience of her mother, of herself, and of her daughter are interconnected from the beginning.

Dr. Bibring calls pregnancy a "normal crisis of growth," like puberty and menopause, in which a woman goes through intense psychological and physiological changes. It is worth remembering that at the center of this process, in which a woman's social identity and status are changed, are biological events—pregnancy and birth. The other two biological transition points of which Bibring speaks take their meaning from their relationship to motherhood: puberty makes a girl capable of becoming a mother, and menopause renders her unable to do so any longer.

Maternity has been so central to the social and sexual definition of women that other aspects of sexual and social identity have, until relatively recently, been almost entirely subordinated to them: sexual repression has been expected of women in the interests of confining birth and maternity to the socially accepted sphere of marriage, and myth has it that after the menopause women are no longer interested in sex. When we consider the importance of childbirth and motherhood in terms of women's social and sexual identity in this culture, it is appalling to realize the extent to which giving birth has become an alienating, even humiliating—and completely nonsexual—experience. This is the message that many, perhaps most, girls and women have received from their mothers about birth, and only recently has it begun to change.

Many women recall their mothers describing pregnancy and childbirth angrily, as though the experience had become part of a mother's reason to resent her own femaleness and perhaps her daughter's as well.

Tina Burgess was thirty when her first child was born. She told me, "Once when Mother was mad at me, she hissed, 'Someday you'll know what it's like to spend nine months of your life with somebody in your stomach, and to go through the most horrible pain you can imagine giving birth to them. You'll know what I put up with to get you!' She couldn't stand to talk about sex, either, so I always just assumed that she hated it. I used to find it hard to imagine her having sex at all.

"I grew up being afraid of childbirth, and I was really surprised to find that I wanted to have children, and that I went ahead and did it, and liked it. It did hurt a lot, but it's a kind of pain that passes very quickly, and having the baby was so wonderful that it seemed worth anything. Maybe natural childbirth made the difference; I think my mother must have been very upset, even mortified, about giving birth at all."

Niles Newton, of Northwestern Medical School, who specializes in the psychology of childbirth, has pointed out the parallels between sexual arousal and orgasm in intercourse and the process that takes place in unanesthetized, natural childbirth.[2] The option to choose natural childbirth, and an increasing emphasis on birth as a positive, sensual, even sexual experience, is giving many women the chance to experience birth differently from the way their mothers did. Not surprisingly, some of these young women discovered a great deal about their sexuality through pregnancy and natural childbirth. Whether or not a woman ever chooses to have children, her feelings about these processes are part of her overall feelings about herself as a woman and as a sexual being. A mother may have given her daughter negative messages about childbirth and sexuality in general, but she is still likely to approve of her daughter's decision to have a child. In the context of natural childbirth, a daughter may find in this approval permission to experience her body for the first time.

"I think I learned the most about my physical self in natural childbirth," Tina recalled. "You learn a lot of things you should know whether you have a child or not. You see what goes on with your body. That's something most mothers don't talk about. It's like getting your period; no one can really tell you what you will experience, yet you can learn a lot so that when it happens nothing shocks you. If even one person had talked to me about childbirth in a positive way,

or just looked happy about it when I was a child it might
have given me a more secure feeling about being a woman.
For my mother, it was very painful; she was nauseous
through the whole pregnancy, and the birth was something
you got knocked out for; it was horrible."

Doris Stern had a similar experience. "Pregnancy was living proof of my femininity. I had always lived so much in
my head. My mother was always very concerned about my
social success; she was very critical of my appearance, and
of anything I did. So I retreated into my head as a refuge
from my conflicts about femininity; I felt very unsure of
myself sexually. When I became pregnant I allowed myself
to feel physical for the first time in my life; I began to masturbate frequently, with lots of fantasies—it was like an
orgy. And giving birth was very sexual, very erotic; I really
did feel almost the same thing as an orgasm at the moment I
pushed the baby out."

Rose Kramer saw natural childbirth in terms of achievement: "I think I separated having babies from sex; birth was
biological, but sex was problematical. My mother's attitude
toward sex was, 'Don't ever let a man touch you, because
men just want to paw and use women.' I got the idea that
women were completely helpless in relation to men, especially in terms of sex. I was very frightened of sex, although
I had always had a very active sex urge. I don't remember a
time in my life when I wasn't masturbating—but by rubbing my legs together, rather than by using my hands.

"I was very frightened of birth, because my mother had
told me it was very painful, and I have a low pain threshold.
I planned to do natural childbirth so I would be completely
in control of it. I considered it a triumph over fear, helplessness, and the whole world of the male authority who tells
you what to do. I had always been passive, but here I was
active; this was the most important thing I was doing in my
life, and I was doing it actively. That was important in terms
of my experience of childbirth and my introduction to motherhood, which for me were totally separate from sex."

The dilemma of a negative image of femaleness and sexuality has been "solved"—although not resolved—by some women who retreat from their sexuality into the world of work and achievement. This is one consequence of society's double message, in which work and achievement are seen as belonging to the realm of men, so that a woman, in entering into this realm, may feel that she has chosen a refuge from femaleness and femininity, with all its attendant implications of vulnerability and even helplessness. But when work is conceived of as an escape from these conflicts, it provides, at best, an imperfect resolution of the problem.

Caroline Lavalle, whom we shall meet again later, said, "I hated the whole idea of being a mother. I hated the birth; it was difficult. I hated the hospital. I didn't believe I would get pregnant; it would not happen to me, so I thought I didn't have to use contraceptives. I thought I wouldn't get pregnant if I was involved in things. I was working, and very involved in thinking about how to be a woman and have a career, and it happened. I was embarrassed; it took me four months to tell anyone at work. I didn't even think about the fact that there was a baby involved. Being pregnant was like a political statement; I had somehow gotten myself into a vulnerable position. It was a real nightmare. But then in a funny way, having a baby gave me an out from the competitiveness of work; I could just do routine things. I think the people at work were glad for me to retire and be a nice adjunct lady. But today I regret not having been able to enjoy my children's birth and their infancies. Infancy was the hardest for me; I was pretty good at it, but I didn't enjoy it."

As Bibring points out, the psychological changes a woman goes through in pregnancy, birth, and the earliest stage of motherhood are vast. She must expand her sense of herself to include a special relationship with the coming child and its meaning in terms of her relationship to herself and to her husband or lover. But perhaps most central to the process is her relationship with her own mother.

The kind of welcome a daughter receives at birth depends partly on her mother's expectations, which, in turn, depend partly on the culture in which they both live. A new mother has ideas and fantasies about the way her daughter ought to be and, perhaps unconsciously, she is readying patterns of behavior and of emotional expectations into which the daughter may or may not fit. She is coming to terms with what the word "mother" means to her, and in so doing she is also creating her own meaning for the word "daughter." She is making decisions about whether to work or not, whether to have natural childbirth or anesthesia, whether to breast-feed or not, that can have important consequences for her relationship with her newborn daughter. The kinds of decisions she makes will reflect her feelings about herself, the demands of her society, and her attitudes toward the baby.

Our society traditionally has prized sons more than daughters; ideally, a mother is supposed to produce a son first, after which it is all right to have a daughter. A son carries on the family name, he is a "gift" to the father from a woman with the right "feminine" attitude—one who is thinking more of her husband's and culture's wishes than of her own. As Helene Deutsch has pointed out, beneath this conscious wish may be a deeper wish for a daughter "in order to be reborn in her, endowed with all the charm of the new being."[3] In talking to pregnant women and new mothers about whether they wanted a son or a daughter, I found that they identified more with daughters than with sons, which is not surprising. What is more interesting is that their wish for a son or daughter seemed to relate strongly to their sense of themselves as women, and to their relationships with their mothers, as Doris's memory makes clear.

"I wanted my first child to be a boy. I think I really was afraid of getting too close to a daughter, and I thought that if she were a boy there would be a definite distance between us. I was afraid that if I had a girl it would just repeat my relationship with my mother. We were so involved with each other, and I had such a hard time breaking away from her, that I just didn't want to inflict that on someone else."

Tina had different reasons for wanting a boy. "It was too horrible to have a girl, because when Jessica was born in 1968, girls didn't have any future. I was sure I was pregnant with a boy and my first child *was* a boy, but I think that someplace deep down I must have wanted to have a girl, because when I did I felt very deeply satisfied. I think partly I was afraid I would have a little girl who was just like I was—timid, physically frail, all those things I can't stand. I was reassured as soon as I saw her; she was big and muscular, and lusty looking. Nothing like me."

However, Rose felt certain from the beginning that she wanted a daughter, partly because she had felt so devalued for being female in her own childhood. "There was no question in my mind that the first child would be a daughter; she had to be. I didn't know what I would do with a son. My whole childhood was geared toward the moment when my mother would have a boy. I grew up thinking that was my father's desire, the Jewish male wanting an heir. When my brother was finally born, dad had a block party. Later I realized that it was actually my mother who wanted a boy all along. She could have said no at any time to more children, but she felt that until she had a boy she had to go right on. A boy would make her a success; until then she was just disappointing my father."

Both Doris and Tina feared having daughters because their sense of themselves as women, and their experience as women in relation to their mothers and to the world, were negative. Rose *wanted* a daughter for just those reasons; as Deutsch suggests, she wanted to be reborn in her daughter into a more positive identity. "I wanted an extension of myself; another me, a happier me, a more successful me. She was going to be a free spirit, noble and courageous, who could make things happen for her the way she wanted them. She would be strong, intelligent, creative, and beautiful—all the things I could not feel about myself. She would make me feel that I had a real connection with the world."

The danger in this kind of fantasizing is, of course, that a mother will overidentify with her daughter, living so intensely through her that she places an impossible burden of expectation on her. As we shall see in the next chapter, this has been and still is a common pattern in mother-daughter relationships. It will change only as women begin to live their own lives, instead of living through the lives of their husbands and children. However, there was a healthy outcome to Rose's fantasy. When she said that she had looked forward to being the mother of a little girl, I asked, "Do you feel mothering a daughter is like reparations, making up to yourself for what you feel didn't exist in your childhood?"

"Absolutely," she replied.

"Do you feel that you have managed to repair some things in yourself, that you suffered in your own childhood?"

"No, but somehow they haven't been important anymore. They stopped being a problem; my childhood stopped being relevant. I guess I just had to grow up. I stopped having to take care of my baby needs. Maybe because I'm taking care of her baby needs the same satisfaction evolves, or the same energy gets used up that's been left over. So you very quickly realize that you have to get rid of those baby needs. It precipitated growth."

Through mothering her daughter, Rose was released from her own infant needs and so from a sense of dependency on her mother.

Pregnancy may become an occasion for a new kind of relationship with a mother: a daughter may become closer to her mother or may even find that she has something in common with her for the first time.

You will recall that Tina was thirty when she got pregnant for the first time. "Being pregnant and giving birth finally gave me something in common with my mother, and that was wonderful," she said. "I had never felt that there was anything in my mother or her life that I really wanted to identify with, but after I became pregnant it seemed like it was smooth sailing with her; when she called up I had something to report, and we had something to talk about for the first time. I was her first daughter to have a child, and she started remembering her own pregnancies. It turned out we both went through nausea in much the same kind of way. It helped me so much to feel close to my mother; it was a woman-to-woman relationship that we didn't have before. It was really outside of her being my mother; she could have been just a friend, except it was maybe more supportive because she was my mother."

Bibring suggests that the new grandmother is able to accept her daughter as an adult because she shifts her emotional investment from her daughter to her grandchild. Doris Stern found that this was true for her. Even though she had been earning her own living for some time, she felt that her relationship with her mother, who was inclined to be critical and demanding, did not change very much until she herself became a mother:

"After my daughter was born there was an intensification of the same kind of relationship we had always had, which was terrible. My mother came to visit me right after she was born; the day after I came home from the hospital. I spent the whole day cleaning. Then after my mother got there she kept saying things like, 'Watch out, you'll drop the baby!' She has always given me the feeling that I was totally incompetent, and my producing a child wasn't any exception. But after a while I think she respected me a little bit more, and she did take some pressure off me. I think what happened was that she started to take more interest in my daughter and less in me. It has been a lot easier for me to get along with her since my daughter was born."

Doris might have had the same experience if her baby had been a boy. For Rose, however, the new personal growth she felt after her baby's birth was related directly to the fact that she had given birth to a girl and could therefore feel that she was taking care of her own baby needs while taking care of her daughter's. Ann Martinson, whom we shall meet again later on, had a different experience. She found that her relationship with her mother at first made her relationship to her new daughter more difficult:

"I was disappointed at my daughter's birth, and I could not figure out why. I've always been very close to my mother and gotten along well with her. All my life I had heard her say she was glad I was a girl because she didn't relate well to little boys. She couldn't be there for my son's birth, and I felt very relaxed with him, and relaxed about being the mother of a boy child. It may be that I felt particularly satisfied at doing something apart from her—and there was no competition in my assumption of motherhood because she had always said she didn't want boys.

"I wanted a girl, too, but when my daughter was born I couldn't relate to her. My mother was there for her birth, and I felt disappointed, angry, and confused. I felt angry at the baby, somehow, and I couldn't figure out why. Then Mother left, and one day I was sick and spent the whole day in bed with the baby, just playing and napping, and it was as if she was born for me on that day; I have felt very close to her ever since. Finally, I realized what it had been: I had really given her to my mother at her birth. I wasn't willing to compete with Mother in an area where I thought she had the experience, and she knew all about mothering girl babies. I simply turned off my daughter instead of my mother."

The fact that new mothers are expected to model their behavior on their own mothers' can create problems because styles of mothering have been changing rapidly in our culture as a whole, and daughters' lives are often very different from those of their mothers.

Denise Howe lives with her husband, an artist, and their two children in a converted warehouse. She told me, "Since my children were born my mother and I are still close, but sometimes we have conflicts. Not that she actually tells me what to do, but she lets me know how she feels, and how she handles things. She never let a child cry, for instance, and I let my daughter cry because I feel she has to learn to be independent. And for my mother, nursing was a necessity; my parents were poor, and we were all born in a lying-in hospital where everyone nursed. Now she asks me why I want to nurse when there is no necessity for it. For her, nursing is a mark of being poor.

"I was definitely overprotected; the atmosphere wasn't geared to letting me figure out things for myself. In my opinion, the hardest thing about being a parent is knowing when to keep hands off. That's one thing I didn't learn from my mother, because if you do it her way you come out with a dependent child. But if you don't accept what was handed down from your mother, you've got nothing. Your head tells you one thing, your body another, your mother something else, and your friends another thing, so finally you just have to make it up."

Denise and a friend of hers discussed some of the complexities of their relationships with their mothers, now that they are mothers themselves. On the one hand, it has made them somewhat closer to their mothers; on the other hand, both have conflicts with their mothers over different styles of mothering. For Denise, the solution is to see herself as more mature than her own mother; she has moved from a level of equality to a sense almost of being, if not her mother's mother, certainly wiser and more forbearing than she is. For her friend Monica Pascoe, this solution has not yet come; she and her mother are still competing over whose style of mothering wins out. Monica is not able to accept her mother's style of mothering, nor is she sufficiently sure of her own style to be able to relax when her mother is around:

"Fortunately for all of us, I live far enough away so that our visits are pleasant because we do love each other. But I find my mother getting insulted when she wants to put a certain powder on my baby's bottom and I tell her I don't use powder; she wails, 'But I always did when you were a baby!' "

"I'm an older mother than you are," said Denise, "and I'm going to say something different. Those are the incidents where you could be more adult than your mother. I went through the same thing with my first child, but with my second I just let them go, because those are the things that are never going to be resolved. I figured, there is no way that she would ever understand my point of view, and it didn't hurt the baby.

"You'd think our mothers would be mature enough to be able to say, 'Well, my daughter doesn't always have her house clean, but that's all right.' But they always want you to do things their way. Realizing that makes it possible to relate to her; I accept the fact that she's not going to understand my point of view, and that it's not absolutely necessary that she does. My mother and I have to try to find the things we agree on, and that isn't always easy. There are a lot of powder incidents, and it took me a long time to realize that I'm sure of myself."

Up until now I have been focusing on the way the new mother's relationship with her own mother affects her attitude toward pregnancy, giving birth, and caring for her new daughter—in other words, how feelings pass from one generation to the next. But with each new birth, a new element is introduced into the chain, and it is not simply a matter of forging a new link out of the existing material. Babies come into the world with their own biology, their particular genes and hormones, possibly with a predisposition to certain kinds of behavior, certain patterns of response. Whether or not they "fit" with their mothers' ideas and predispositions will make a difference.

At first an infant's social identity exists in its mother and its mother's culture. As the baby and mother start to relate to each other, a complex web will be spun out of their interactions. All infants begin by perceiving themselves as, literally, part of the mother. This stage of symbiosis, when an infant sees no difference between itself and its mother, lasts for about the first six months of life, during which a strong attachment to the mother is formed. After this, if the mother

is neither rejecting nor overly possessive, she will allow her
baby to begin separating itself from her and to become
aware that there is an "I" and a "you."[4] The child's sense
that she possesses a separate self evolves slowly. By the age
of three, however, it is thought that a child will have developed a clear sense of self and nonself, and of his or her gender.
With few exceptions, this concept of the evolving self has
not—in psychoanalytic theory at least—looked closely at the
evolution of daughters as opposed to sons.[5] But there are
many indications to suggest that not only is the social concept of self different for men and women, but that daughters
tend to stay more closely involved with their mothers' identities—that to some extent they never achieve a clear sense
of a separate self at all. In the next chapter we shall look at
some of the ways in which mothers are trying to change this
situation; here, we shall look at some of the ways in which a
daughter's identity is molded by her earliest relationship
with her mother.

For the sake of clarity, I have divided identity into three
aspects: personal identity, sexual identity, and gender or sex-
role identity, which I shall call gender identity. They are all
related, but it is useful to try to see them clearly in their
separate aspects. Personal identity is a woman's sense of herself as a separate individual, with a sense of autonomy in her
activities and in her relationships with other people. Sexual
identity refers to a woman's identity as a biological female,
and how comfortable she feels with her body and its sexuality. Gender identity is a woman's idea of herself as a female
in society; the ways in which she learns to identify herself as
a woman, or as "feminine." Gender identity includes such
relatively superficial things as clothing and hair styles, and
more fundamental personality aspects such as the way a
woman behaves toward men and toward other women.

Personal identity, the sense of self, is the earliest to evolve,
although it soon becomes interrelated with increasing
awareness of sexual and gender identity. As Dr. Marjorie
Taggart White, a psychologist and psychoanalyst, put it,

babies are aware of whether or not they are respected as separate people before they are aware of their identities as males or females.[6] But respect for the separateness of females has never been very great, and it may be that this most basic aspect of identity has not usually been encouraged in girls.

Mothers of daughters are daughters of mothers and have remained so, in circles joined to circles, since time began. They are bound together by a shared destiny. Daughters have been expected simply to assume the identity of their mothers, "naturally" growing up to become wives and mothers in their "own right." The sense of biological inevitability underlying this expectation has been taken for granted by both sexes until quite recently; in fact, the generation of daughters now growing up may be the first one in history to feel that motherhood can be one choice among many that a woman can make.

But there is also a psychological inevitability about this line of development. If daughters are expected to assume the identity of their mothers, there is no reason for them to achieve a sense of separate self. Nancy Chodorow, a sociologist at the University of California at Santa Cruz, has pointed out that women everywhere are defined by their relationships—to their husbands, their mothers, their children, and so forth. Men, on the other hand, are defined as individuals.[7] This is the main way in which the concept of self is different for men and women. The psychologist David Gutmann has suggested that this very tendency to live in and through other people—to behave as though there were no difference between self and other—is an essential part of being a good mother.[8] But Chodorow disagrees. She feels that a mother's inability to differentiate clearly between herself and her child may be particularly destructive to a daughter's development.

To an infant, the mother is the environment. Cultural expectations of femininity are first conveyed to daughters by their mothers, at first in ways so subtle that they have only recently begun to be detected. Girls in our society have been expected to be less assertive, more dependent, to have greater self-control and more sexual inhibitions than boys. All of these qualities contribute to a girl's developing less of a sense of herself and more of a sense of depending on other people than is expected of a boy.

At the same time, the early relationship of mothers and infants is an interaction in which each is adapting to the other. Arguments about how much of a baby's behavior is innate and how much is molded by a mother's expectations continue to rage, but at least two sex-related differences have been widely agreed upon. One is that male infants are more irritable and less well-coordinated than female infants. In different studies, psychologists Howard A. Moss and Michael Lewis found that in the early months of life male infants were held more than female infants, after which the reverse was true; mothers spent less time holding their sons and more time encouraging them to be active.[9] Moss speculates that baby girls are more easily soothed than baby boys because they are physiologically and neurologically better coordinated. They may demand less physical soothing at first, but they respond to it better, encouraging the mother to continue cuddling them.

The second major difference is that baby girls, as Lewis points out, are more sensitive to the things they hear than are baby boys. Both Moss and Lewis agree that infant girls are talked to more than infant boys.

Starting in early infancy, then, girls are apparently more responsive to being physically soothed and talked to by their mothers than boys are, which immediately involves them in a closer relationship with their mothers.

Mothering is a complicated function. In most people's minds it is associated with the idea of nurturing and protecting children, who are to some degree helpless and dependent. But there is another, more positive, aspect of mothering that involves support for a child's developing autonomy. This might be called "enabling," in which a mother encourages a child to grow and develop as an individual in her own right. [10] This is what we expect mothers to do for their sons; we are only beginning to realize that it is not usually done for daughters. And a mother who has not received the support to enable her to develop a sense of autonomy is likely to cling to the nurturing, protective aspect of mothering in relation to her daughter, who is thus encouraged to remain dependent, with a diffuse sense of self.

On the other hand, girls are encouraged to "socialize" more than boys, to "chatter" with their mothers while their little brothers are out "doing" things, and this early interpersonal involvement helps them develop a capacity for deep relationships with other people. Boys, in the process of becoming self-assertive and independent, develop a more rigid personal identity that may inhibit close ties with other people.

The problem many new mothers are facing is how to help their daughters develop a strong sense of self, so that they don't grow up expecting to "lose themselves" in relationships with other people because they never "found themselves" in their relationships with their mothers. Like Denise and Monica, they are finding that they must, as Denise said, make up their own styles of mothering. But the culture in which they were raised continues to carry explicit and implicit instructions for them and their daughters about what motherhood and daughterhood ought to be. Young mothers are beginning to change their modes of mothering and their ways of relating to their daughters, but this does not happen without some conflict and perhaps confusion.

Denise's daughter, Hannah, is now one year old. "As yet I don't feel myself behaving like my mother did toward me. I feel a strong relationship with Hannah as a person; I felt that from the beginning. I felt as if I was the receptacle for her to be born through. There are so many things about her that I didn't plan, and so many things that I don't know; I think babies are born with certain definite temperaments. From the beginning she was crying, awake a lot, and very energetic. Her body is hard, whereas a lot of little girls' bodies are soft. Her temperament is very different from mine; I avoid conflict, and I don't cry or show emotion very much. I like the way she is, so I'm very sure I've encouraged it, but I think she had her own distinct personality from the beginning.

"A lot of people think she's a boy when they first see her. For one thing, she still doesn't have much hair, and people associate hair with girls. And she wears blue, because she wears her older brother's leftovers. And she's more aggressive than other girls her age. I don't really think of her in terms of gender yet; she will play with anything—dolls, trucks, pots and pans. I'm very conscious of the pitfalls of the 'nice girl' syndrome—that's what my mother tried to make me, and I've spent most of my adult life trying not to be a nice girl. I think you can give kids toys that aren't really gender-related—for instance, natural toys, rather than fire engines or dolls."

Ironically, the confusion here does not lie with Denise or Hannah but with society, with the people who have difficulty accepting this energetic little person as a girl. On the other hand, Monica is ambivalent about what she expects of her daughter: "I had planned not to raise her 'feminine,' but I discovered that I enjoy dressing her up, and I thought, 'Wait a minute, that's not how I planned it.' I am sort of coming to the conclusion that I want her to have the same opportunities that my son has, to realize that she can do whatever she wants, but I think that there are differences between boys and girls, and you can play around with it, have a good time with it. I want her to rough and tumble, I don't want any restrictions on her behavior. But at the same time she can wear ruffles and get away with it, if she feels like it. I'm having fun dressing her now, because I figure that in another year or two she'll be out in the sandbox, and she won't want to wear dresses anyway. But there is one difference: she can wear ruffles, but society would probably laugh at my son if he did.

"My son is three; he has dolls, but doesn't look at them. He loves all the stereotyped masculine things. My daughter is only eight months old, and she's everything you think is supposed to be feminine. She flirts and smiles. She's also much calmer, much easier to have around. My son is always on the move. I think she has a given personality; she's very strong, so she's not going to be just sitting there. But I had expected them to be more alike as babies."

Monica says that she wants to give her daughter the opportunity to grow up without feminine restrictions, and yet when the little girl laughs and babbles, her mother calls the behavior flirtatious. She would never have applied such a label to her son's similar baby moods. In the following chapters we shall explore the implications these kinds of conflicting messages hold for daughters.

II

CULTURE AND THE
SEPARATE SELF

One day I was walking in a city park with a West Indian woman, a grandmother who now takes care of someone else's child. Running ahead of us was a group of neighborhood children we had collected on our way to the park, simply because Pat enjoys children and they universally love her. I asked Pat whether she thought it was harder to raise girls today than it had been when her daughter was growing up in Jamaica. She laughed and said, "Yes, and I'll tell you why. I'm sixty-five years old and I'm very much like my mother. You're thirty-three and you're quite a bit different from your mother, but you're also like her in many ways. But these children"—and she pointed to the group of preschoolers, most of whom happened to be girls—"they're different altogether. Who knows who they're going to be like? They only take after themselves."

As I talked to mothers of preschool daughters about their own mothers, about their lives and their ways of mothering their daughters, I often thought about Pat's remark. Gradually, it began to seem to me that a revolution of sorts is in the making. Every generation has wished for a better life for its children, but many mothers with small daughters today seem determined to alter, by the very patterns of their mothering, the nature of the mother–daughter relationship and the ways in which their daughters define themselves as girls and women. Not all mothers are trying to do this; the ones who are have usually been affected to some degree by feminism. Many of them are responding to newly felt demands to undertake some work that establishes them as persons in their own right, in addition to their roles as mothers and wives. Whether they work or not, their attitude toward themselves has changed. Perhaps the main difference between them and previous generations of mothers is that the latter defined themselves primarily as mothers even when they worked. Mothers of young children today see motherhood as part of their identity, but not the whole of it. They are trying to construct a style of mothering in which their own needs as persons are not submerged in the needs of their families and in which the identities of their children, and particularly of their daughters, are not subordinated to their expectations.

This is the essence of what many mothers refer to as the new motherhood; the mothers who are evolving it are the subject of this chapter. They are the mothers who are struggling to work out methods of child care that take into consideration the needs of both their families and themselves. In this, their main allies are other mothers; society as a whole offers little support, whether in alternative images of mothering or in facilities for child care. Mothers who are evolving the new motherhood must struggle with added burdens of guilt at laying aside not only their own mothers' styles of mothering but also the strictures of our whole culture, including the advice of many child-care specialists. In addition to coping with the responsibilities of motherhood they must deal with their own, often quite new, demands on themselves as individuals. One of the biggest generation gaps in history may be in the making; like the children of immigrants, who created their own identities in a new culture, many mothers are creating, as adults, new identities for themselves and—they hope—for their daughters.

This generation of middle-class mothers of preschool children was, by and large, raised in upwardly mobile families who were themselves determined that their daughters should not only finish high school but go on to college. After college their fate was to be that of girls of all classes: marriage and a family. Their mothers were the women called "Mom," whose relationship to their sons has been analyzed and criticized by writers from Philip Wylie to Philip Roth, but whose relationship to their daughters has gone largely unnoticed, except by Margaret Mead in *Male and Female*[1] and, briefly, by Erik Erikson in *Childhood and Society*.[2] Mom may have worked, but she usually gave it up when she had children. Uncomfortable with her own sexuality, she nevertheless may have believed intellectually that sex was nothing to be ashamed of. Having no alternatives to the role of mother, she sacrificed herself for her children, passing on to her daughter, in the form of double messages, her own confusion about sexuality and her ambivalence about her role as mother. She educated her daughter carefully in femininity, as she herself had been educated; at the same time, influenced by new ideas and styles in child rearing, she may have allowed her daughter considerable physical freedom, sometimes to the point of tomboyishness if the daughter wished. But physical freedom did not extend to overt displays of sexuality such as masturbation or "playing doctor," which were frowned on or even punished. (The sons of Mom were under the same restrictions, but, again, the repercussions have been commented upon more frequently for boys than for girls.) Most of Mom's energy was channeled into mothering; she inherited an image of the ideal mother that she tried to live up to, having no other model for her life.

The daughters of Mom came of age in the sexual revolution, having had childhoods that hardly prepared them for the new bodily freedom that was offered them. They are armed with knowledge of at least some of the vast literature of psychology and child development that has proliferated in the last twenty or thirty years, and they are determined to raise their daughters differently from the way they were raised.

Joyce Calisher lives in an airy city apartment with her husband and daughter, Carol, who is three-and-a-half. Joyce is very consciously trying to alter the pattern of mothering she received; together with several other mothers, she started a day-care center when Carol was eighteen months old. Carol has been attending the center regularly, and Joyce has remained deeply involved with the center. At first she took turns with the other mothers as a teacher. Since the center has been approved for government funding, a professional staff is now required, but Joyce continues to work actively with the parent governing board, and her interest in day care has motivated her to work for a doctorate in developmental psychology. She offers this description of the contrast between traditional mothering and the new motherhood:

"I have two images of motherhood; one is the ideal mother, and one is more realistic. The ideal is a mother who is totally present, totally devoted to her children and her family, totally unselfish in that everyone else's needs come first. Her energy is spent in creating a home where everyone, kids and husband, feel well loved and secure. She never complains. She also has some life of her own, she is involved in the community, which is seen as an extension of the home." Joyce's ideal mother sounds a lot like Mom.

"The second image reflects my own reality. I think a mother has to be more in touch with her own needs, apart from children, apart from other people. If I'm comfortable with what I need and what I want, I feel I can provide more for my daughter than by denying myself. And even when I say, 'Look, I can't play with you, I have a whole lot of things on my mind'—it's hard, but I can say it. It's a developing thing. With Carol, some things come first, and there's no way to work that out. I'm an adult, I can put things off, but a child isn't always capable of that. But it's getting to the point where we can balance out the times when we're apart and the times when we're together, and both of us accept it."

The image of the ideal mother is tenacious, even when it is recognized as more of a myth than the reality of a mother's own childhood. Ellen Barbour is a mother in her thirties who has managed to maintain both a marriage and a successful career in advertising. Her daughter, Sally, is four-and-a-half. Ellen says, "I find that there are things I want Sally to remember. We do a lot of cooking together, and I find I really want her to remember me as this sort of motherly figure that I remember my mother being—although she wasn't either, she sat around most of the time, but she did every now and then whip up a little cinnamon roll or something. And I just loved those things; I loved to watch her, and to help her, and I loved—just the whole thing about it. All kids seem to love it, and I really want Sally to have that. Although it's ludicrous to come racing in from the subway and immediately start baking bread, which takes until two in the morning."

There is another face to the ideal mother; it is the mother who needs to control her children because her main source of power lies in the family. Guilt is one of her great weapons. Yvonne Glascock, a separated mother who is working full-time as a high school teacher while raising her five-year-old daughter Vicki recalls that, "Whatever I did reflected completely on my mother. If I was successful, then it meant that she felt she was great. Anything I did was a personal act directed at her."

Yvonne is struggling to free herself from a binding relationship with her own mother that seems to contain equal parts of love and hate. She is trying not to fall into the trap of the ideal mother, who, to the extent that she is trying to live up to an image of perfection is likely to demand perfection in her children. But Yvonne's problem is that on some level she thinks she *ought* to be living up to that image, and she expressed this conflict in talking about her relationship with Vicki:

"When she does something, like being silly when I want her to take something seriously, I feel this anger rising up in me. I really do feel that I'd like to be able to control her. But I know I can't. And then I realize this whole issue is flowing from the way I was brought up. I would like her to be a model little person, right? And sometimes I have trouble dealing with that. The imperfection of it all, the unpredictability of it all. I have a lot of hangups about living up to things, and I don't think it's fair to inflict that on her. Although I'm sure she must sense it."

Ideal mothers want ideal daughters, because so much of their identity is bound up in what they "make" of their daughters, and traditionally they have been expected to feel that their daughters' behavior reflected directly on them. But there are other aspects of the problem of separating that may come simply from the fact that daughters are daughters. The psychologist David B. Lynn, of the University of California, and others have pointed out that little girls may have a particularly difficult time separating from their mothers because they are of the same sex, and therefore identify most deeply with the very person from whom they must psychologically separate themselves.[3] As discussed in Chapter I, all infants at first perceive themselves as part of the mother. Growth in the early years involves gradually breaking away from this symbiotic relationship, a process in which boys may be helped by the fact that their primary identification is shifted to the father.

Also, as we have seen, it is from mothers that daughters first learn what is expected of them as females in society, what "femininity" is. In our culture femininity implies dependency, nonassertiveness, and a tendency to live in and through others—to rely more on relationships than on one's sense of oneself.

Messages about behavioral expectations received in the

earliest years are crucial in the development of personality. Not surprisingly, psychologists Jerome Kagan and Howard A. Moss, in a study of a group of children from infancy to adulthood, found that strictness and protectiveness by mothers in early childhood tended to produce passive and dependent daughters by rewarding dependent behavior and discouraging or even punishing independence.[4] Protectiveness toward small girls was found to be closely correlated with passive, dependent behavior in those same girls when they grew up. Conversely, a certain amount of "maternal hostility"—what Lois Hoffman, a psychologist at the University of Michigan, calls "the absence of smother love"—was found to produce girls who, as women, were more able to tolerate the stress and frustration of independent behavior.[5]

Dependency has played a particular part in the social role of women; the daughter who remains dependent on her mother will transfer her dependency to her husband and will expect her daughter to be dependent on her, repeating the cycle. Training in femininity, then, works against a small girl's development of a sense of her own identity; submerged in her mother's identity, she will naturally be close to her, but the closeness will not be that of two people interrelating. It will be the closeness of two people who are more nearly one person, who do not quite know where each ends and the other begins.

Too often, the relationship between a daughter and her mother remains in that unresolved state in which a mother never quite manages to let go of her daughter, and the daughter never quite manages to break free of her infantile dependency on her mother. To some extent, she will relive through her daughter both her own childhood self and her mother's identity as she absorbed it in childhood; she will become both her own mother and her own child.

Nancy Chodorow suggests that mothers in our society have an investment in keeping girls infantile because they themselves have neither a clear sense of self nor an opportunity to develop an investment of energies in anything except other people, specifically, their children.[6] Sons may also experience this "boundary confusion," but they are offered some protection through identification with their fathers and through role expectations. Chodorow suggests that, in a context in which a mother's life is not so sharply circumscribed, it may be possible for daughters to develop more sense of self—and of self-assertiveness—without at the same time having to forfeit their capacity for deep, close relationships. She cites matrifocal cultures in which women have real, functional economic responsibility within the group. These women, she suggests, have no stake in keeping their daughters infantile. At the same time, daughters grow up observing their mothers and other women in a variety of contexts. Because the women in these cultures have functioning roles beyond child rearing, there are external factors that limit the extreme emotional involvement that seems to be more common among mothers and daughters in our society.

In 1950 Erik Erikson predicted that the crisis for the daughters of Mom would come when, as mothers confronting their own small daughters, they would find themselves reexperiencing their infantile identifications with their own mothers.[7] Ellen has found that this is all too true: "Sally seems to be a combination of my mother and myself, in this person who is also very unique. When I have very emotional conversations with her, I usually find myself sort of acting my mother's part out with her, even my mother's words or her tone of voice. Sometimes the part of Sally that I'm talking to is the part that's most like my mother, and then I'll suddenly begin to feel a lot like myself as a child—it's very weird. I seem to be working a lot of things out through her, in terms of my mother, and myself as a child. The one missing person is me as an adult."

"What do you mean when you say you're missing? Aren't you a person in this situation too?" I asked.

"But that's what I don't really have a strong sense of, when I deal with Sally. What comes out when I just start yelling at her is either myself at a much earlier age, or my mother."

"How are you working things out through her, then?"

"One big part of it is trying to get back in touch with myself, the way I was then—because I still don't understand why I did the things I did, and I guess I'm trying to find out through her a lot of the time, trying to figure out what's different between me and Sally, how she deals with something that I would have dealt with in a different way."

Ellen clearly is trying to gain some perspective on her relationship with her daughter. A daughter's view of a mother who was apparently unable to do so was expressed at a feminist workshop on motherhood by a woman who recalled bitterly, "All my life my mother was three years old, and I was expecting her to be an adult. If I had known she was only three years old I wouldn't have expected so much from her."

On the other hand, if a mother feels caught up in her own childhood difficulties through her involvement with her daughter, it is sometimes possible to set these problems to rights instead of simply remaining embroiled. Some women have the ability to "make up" for their own childhood problems by nurturing daughters. One social worker who is also a mother described her own mother as very distant; she feels that by establishing a warmer relationship with her daughters she is giving both them and herself the mothering she never had.

Kate Pulaski is the mother of a five-year-old daughter and a seven-year-old son. She is struggling with the problems of establishing a career as a free-lance journalist while raising her children, and appears to be on the verge of separating from her husband because she finds him unable or unwilling either to participate in child care so she can work, or to provide emotional support for her efforts. As she begins to take her work seriously, she finds herself having to deal with her negative feelings toward herself, feelings that originated in early childhood, in her relationship with her mother. Kate finds that "having a girl is quite therapeutic for me, because my relationship with her is so different from my mother's relationship with me. It's like making up."

"How does that work?" I asked.

"I think partly she's acting out a lot of parts of me that I've never been able to express myself. She's very unimpressed by adult authority; I just wasn't brought up like that. And she's always been very physical. She fights back physically; I was always afraid to. She seems to be much more daring than I was. Also, she looks quite different from the way I did as a child. I'm glad she doesn't have the kind of hair I have, and she doesn't look the way I do."

If Kate's daughter looked like her, or were more like her in style and temperament, Kate might not be able to get as much pleasure out of the relationship. Ellen feels that the fact that Sally looks and acts a lot like she did at the same age makes it more difficult to relate to her as a separate person. Mothers who are comfortable with themselves as persons have expressed great pleasure in relating to daughters who, they feel, are a lot like them. In order to loosen the circle, to allow and even encourage her daughter to become a separate, independent person, a mother must separate herself psychologically from her own mother; only then can she separate herself from her daughter as well.

As Joyce's description implied, mothers who are evolving the new motherhood are trying to separate their power as mothers from what might be called personal power. The daughters of Mom perceive their mothers to be very powerful *as mothers*, and often are painfully aware that they have made only a partial separation from them. Thus they have an incomplete sense of themselves as persons in their own right. Paradoxically, however, they feel that *as persons* their mothers often felt weak and even helpless, and that they were full of rage that expressed itself in the ambivalent message that they passed on to their daughters. This paradox is well expressed by the different views of Mom held by Betty Friedan in *The Feminine Mystique* and by Philip Wylie in

Generation of Vipers.[8] Wylie, writing as Mom's son, perceived her as powerful, castrating, all-engulfing. Friedan, approaching Mom as a person, saw that she felt herself to be impotent, trapped in a domestic box in which her energies and potential were allowed few outlets.

Because they are of the same sex, the daughters of Mom have had a different problem from the sons. Daughters identify with their mothers, and thus these daughters absorbed Mom's confusion about herself. They often resent both Mom's power over them in her role as mother and the weak image of herself as a person that she conveyed to them. They do not want to burden their daughters with the same necessity to live up to their expectations as mothers while also, somehow, living out their repressed desires and needs as persons. The daughters of Mom are trying to evolve their own identities as persons, thereby reducing their own need for mother power in their relationships with their daughters. They would like their daughters to have the chance to be persons from the beginning; they want them above all to be strong, separate personalities, ready and able to deal with the real world.

Joyce expressed her feelings in terms of the double message she received from her mother: "I want Carol to be straightforward, and to be able to stand up for herself. I want her to be direct; I don't want her to rely on submission to get by. Not only is that something we've been forced into, but it's also a cop-out. I guess I want her to be an honest person, and to be able to do what she wants, and decide what she wants, to have the opportunities to do what she wants but also within herself to be able to act. My mother never had a career, but she's always been involved with community organizations. She's a very forceful person. At the same time, though, she put my father through law school by being a secretary, and I just grew up assuming that I was going to be a secretary."

As their conceptions of themselves and their daughters

change, the new mothers are inevitably rethinking their attitudes toward relationships between men and women. In fact,
the very idea that women can have a sense of self is a
comparatively new one. The idea of self has been associated
in our culture with males. So, too, the idea of achieving in
the world is identified with the masculine role. Even today,
most women who are achievers think of themselves as identifying more with their fathers' role than with their mothers'.
But the new mothers are particularly concerned with identifying "self" and "achievement" as *feminine*, so that their
daughters will not need to feel that they must become "like
men" in order to become separate selves. The choice need
not be between rigid overdefinition of self and extreme im-
beddedness of self in relationships. There is a third possibility, which demands the molding of personality of both boys
and girls in different directions—toward more independence
in girls, and toward more interdependency in boys.

A new sense of independent selfhood means less dependence on male approval. Kate feels strongly that she would
like to help her daughter Ann develop such a sense of herself, so that she will be able to deal with the world of men
and women more nearly on her own terms, with less of the
pain Kate recalls in growing up with a belief that her self-
esteem depended largely on pleasing men. She told me that
"boys have always had a certain place in this world, and
girls have had a certain place. But I want Ann to have more
opportunity than I had. I want her to have a different view-
point on the world, and a different way of operating in this
world than I did. I feel I can have more to say about that
with a daughter than I can with a son. My son is seven, and
already it's as if I'm not really part of his world anymore.
But with Ann I feel like, 'Here's a chance.' She was born
before I got involved with feminism, but even then I
thought, 'She's going to know more, she's going to be able to
make choices.' Because of the way society is, my son doesn't
have that problem. If he's a strong person and able to ex-

press himself, knows what he wants, he can do it. But a mother has a special part in shaping her daughter's view of the world."

John Money, a professor of medical psychology at Johns Hopkins Hospital who has worked for many years with hermaphrodites—people who are born with ambiguous genital organs—frequently has discussed the powerful effects of environmental conditioning on infants and small children.[9] A girl born without a vagina, or even with a rudimentary penis or enlarged clitoris, will, if her parents definitely "assign" her as a girl and treat her accordingly, grow up feeling certain of her gender identity. In one case, a baby born genetically, hormonally, and physically male was accidentally castrated while being circumcised. After consultation with a doctor, the baby was "reassigned" as a girl; the mother began dressing her in frilly clothing and let her hair grow, and the child became much neater and more concerned about cleanliness than her twin brother. She was allowed less freedom than he; if she took her underpants off outside, she was told it wasn't "nice," whereas her brother was allowed to urinate in the garden. The mother explained the advantages of being female in terms of having babies (although, of course, this child will never be able to do so), and encouraged her daughter to copy her in domestic work. The girl wanted dolls for presents and by the age of five-and-a-half had "feminine" plans for the future, including marriage and a career as a doctor or teacher, while her brother wanted to be a policeman or fireman.

Nothing could illustrate the influence of gender-role training more completely than this case, in which hormones, genes, and biology apparently were completely overridden: told that she was a girl, the child became a girl.

After an infant is about eighteen months old, Dr. Money notes, such sex reassignment becomes psychologically very difficult because a baby has absorbed too much information about its role identity. He believes that ordinarily extreme gender-role differentiation isn't necessary: "It doesn't matter if father cooks the dinner and mother drives the tractor . . . so long as there are clear boundaries delineating, at a minimum, the reproductive and erotic roles of the sexes." Yet a clear sense of gender identity is not enough; the extent of real autonomy a child develops will relate to issues of control and freedom.

The new mothers are thinking in terms of their daughters' personal identity rather than simply their gender identity. They seem more concerned about helping their daughters develop a generalized base of independent personality rather than attempting to mold specific alternative gender-role behaviors, and in this their instincts are sound. A mother can be just as controlling and intrusive in trying to get her daughter to play with trucks instead of dolls as any stereotyped Mom may be in insisting that her daughter wear a certain frilly dress and keep it clean. The more superficial aspects of gender roles are less important than a child's sense that she is respected as a separate person. This involves the sense that she has the freedom to make choices, within reasonable limits and on her own level. It means that she has a sense that she owns her body, that she is free to explore and experience the pleasures it provides her, that the control of its functions belongs to her and not to her mother, and that she is unambivalently encouraged to use her body in developing competence in physical activities and in exploring the world. It means that she is allowed to develop emotional independence; that her feelings are acknowledged and respected as belonging to her and are not seen by adults, particularly her mother, as threatening.

One way that Joyce encourages Carol to assert her independence is by permitting her to make choices. Joyce recalls that her own mother insisted on picking out her clothes every day. It was important to her mother that Joyce look "just right," because Joyce's appearance reflected her sense of herself as a successful mother, a role in which most of her sense of herself as a person was bound up. Carol, at three-and-a-half, chooses her own clothes.

"It's really hard for me," Joyce relates, "because of the way it was for me. I'll say, 'It doesn't match.' Carol will say, 'Yes it does match; this is red and this is pink.' Well, what the hell if it doesn't match, that's what she wants to wear." A small thing, perhaps, but Joyce links her daughter's ability to make choices on this level, at this age, to a developing sense of confidence in her own ability to make choices that reflect her own ideas, rather than Joyce's. Joyce recalls her own mother as by no means overprotective; nevertheless, "I was very tied up in her." As a young adult, Joyce recalls, she would call her mother constantly to ask her opinion about decisions, even on whether she had chosen the right engagement ring! "I wanted to know that what I was thinking was all right; I wanted her to tell me."

So far, Joyce is pleased with the results of her attempts to give Carol plenty of room for choice within limits: "She's really an incredibly responsible person. She's very independent, but she's not stubborn, so we don't get into power fights. But," she added ruefully, "the result of her independence is that sometimes she can give me a whole lot of reasons why she's doing something I don't particularly like."

Small children of both sexes need to develop a sense of physical autonomy in a secure and loving emotional context, but it may be particularly important for girls to receive encouragement in discovering the possibilities of their bodies. Then they can realize that, although they are like their mothers, they own their own bodies, bodies that have their own potential and their own capacities for movement, exploration, and achievement.

Margaret Mahler, a psychoanalyst whose theory of separation and individuation was mentioned in the last chapter, points out that the toddler's pleasure in her new independence is proportionate to the degree to which she can gain her mother's interest and participation in her activity.[10] With this support she gains a sense that her increasing separation from her mother is "all right," which lays the foundation for later confidence in herself as an individual.

It is probable, however, that mothers are likely to give their daughters less support for their new achievements than they do their sons. Lois Hoffman suggests that if a mother responds to her daughter's first steps with anxiety—and mothers have been shown to think of daughters as more fragile than sons despite the fact that daughters are usually better coordinated—the child will get the message that she is perhaps not quite competent. This lack of encouragement, together with the fact that a daughter may separate herself from her mother later and less completely than a son because she is of the same sex, plus a tendency for girls to have fewer conflicts with their parents than boys do, all combine to make girls less confident in themselves as individuals. Instead of coping directly with the world, Hoffman suggests, girls tend to rely more on their relationships with people for a sense of safety and as a way of feeling they have an effect on the world. This shows up in a greater tendency for girls to be dependent, and a cycle is set up in which girls, never discovering the pleasures of achievement, competency, and mastery, remain "feminine"—and nonachieving.[11]

The emphasis on gender roles in our society has tended to obscure this point. There is an absurd but somehow deeply felt conviction that girls who are allowed physical independence will not only "act like boys" but will want to be boys, will grow up rejecting both their feminine roles and their essential sexual identity. This is a complex issue, relating in part to the misconception that gender identity is the same thing as personal and sexual identity. As we shall see in the next chapter, biologically normal girls get information about themselves from their bodies that, if not repressed because of negative reactions from their environment to their desires to explore and experience their bodies, will help reinforce their sense of sexual identity. In Money's example, rather rigid gender-role training was probably essential in the social development of a child whose body would, at best, provide it with extremely ambiguous information. But normal girls who are given considerable physical freedom may be less likely to want to be boys than those who appear more passive.

Sally has never been in a playpen. She was fond of climbing ladders before she could walk, and she has always had great freedom to explore her own body, her house, and her neighborhood. At four-and-a-half she loves dancing and swimming, and will frequently toss off her underpants when playing outside. When I asked her what she wanted to do when she grew up, her first response was "work," only after which came, "have babies." At the same time, she is deeply involved with some of the stereotyped attributes of femininity; she loves dresses, jewelry, and makeup, which she demands for presents—somewhat to the bemusement of her mother, who frequently wears pants, seldom wears jewelry, and feels she has never tried to influence Sally in the direction of traditional feminine roles. Yet, Ellen says, "Sally has always been fearless and aggressive because she has always had a lot of physical freedom."

"She doesn't feel any conflict between being aggressive and being a girl?" I asked.

"No. She's much more aggressive than any kid she knows, including boys. She'll walk up to people and say, 'Hi, my name is Sally,' and start talking to them. She'll go up and hit somebody six years old without blinking. She has a dear friend who refuses to wear a skirt, but who is not aggressive at all. She is very sweet and retiring and really just wants to sit on somebody's lap. She is much more feminine in the classic sense of passive, or whatever, than Sally is, but if you ask her she will say she wants to be a boy."

Emotional independence is less easy to define than physical independence, but it is equally crucial. A mother's emotions can have a powerful effect on a daughter and can become part of the glue that binds a daughter to her mother from guilt and fear. Small children tend to relate everything that happens around them to themselves, and when a mother explodes in rage, or cries, a little girl will think she's responsible. If she is not allowed to express her own feelings, a daughter will be that much less sure of who she is, of whether it is all right to have her own emotions.

Yvonne described vividly her own experience, and how she is trying to stop the cycle: "I do try to get Vicki to express her feelings; to me that's the biggest legacy I could give her. And I do try to tell her how I feel, because I grew up in a home where my mother used to say to me, 'You mustn't say you hate anybody.' I'd say, 'I hate you!' and she'd say, 'Don't ever use that word to me!' Well, I did hate her, but it was as though I were killing her. 'You're killing me!' There was a lot of guilt there; I always felt that I had done something terrible. And my mother would get into these rages, and then she would cry, and then she would lock herself in her room. And I would bang on the door and say, 'Let me in, Mother, let me in!' She would say, 'No, go away, go away!' And I would always feel so forlorn, so lost. I wanted her to tell me it was all right. I was always asking my mother, 'Do you love me?' 'Of course I love you. How could you doubt it?' Well, hell, I did doubt it. She was rejecting me.

"When I get angry with Vicki, I explode. And her face sort of shrivels up. I always reach out for her then, and hold her, and I always say, 'Mommy got angry,' and she says, 'I was scared.' And I say, 'Yes, I know. Mommy sometimes loses her temper. I should try to do it some other way, but sometimes you lose your temper too.' I try to let her know that I know that she's frightened, because I was terrified when my mother got angry; it means rejection, it means abandonment. I guess the whole thing is really just being sensitive to her as a person. I remember that I thought of her as a little person, and I always say, 'little person' to her, because she's a person, and she has feelings. I can't use her as a whipping post for my frustrations, which is what my mother did to me, totally without awareness of what she was doing. To explode the way she did was terrifying because she was losing control of herself."

Nurturing care by, and interaction with, adults other than her mother may provide a means for a daughter to begin to separate herself from her mother and to gain a clearer sense of her own identity. Day care and other alternative forms of stable, nurturing child care may be particularly important for girls. Of course, physical separation of a daughter and mother does not necessarily guarantee emotional separation; in fact, if separation comes too soon or is too great, exactly the opposite result is likely to occur. But most mothers who are involved in cooperative, community-oriented day-care programs are not buying the current wisdom of child-care specialists that any separation between mother and child before the age of three is necessarily harmful. At least one study found that attachment between mothers and children involved in a day-care program from the time the children were a year old was as strong as that between mothers and children who stayed home together.[12] Another study suggests that by the age of eighteen months most infants are capable of forming strong subsidiary attachments while still retaining a primary tie to the mother.[13]

Joyce described her feelings about the separation involved in day care: "The hardest thing about separating was that somewhere in me was still the need for Carol to be totally dependent on me and to think I could do no wrong. I think somewhere in me there was still a wanting to be idolized and idealized. As it keeps going, it makes much more sense to me to be humanized. But that's where the guilt came in. A lot of times I thought, 'My God, what am I doing? I'm trying to create something new but it could be a million times worse. If I'm not spending time with her, it's damaging to her.' And that was hard, really trusting that the experiences she was having away from me were important and positive, and I didn't have to be doing it all myself, my creation." But Joyce felt that it was important that, "Somehow my identity wouldn't depend on how she turned out, and what our relationship was. She was going to be the result of lots of different things, although strongly what we did together."

A visit to Carol's day-care center was instructive; the children had in no sense been abandoned. Carol ran to her mother, welcomed her, confided in her, and was then eager to return to her friends and activities. The center was a warm, pleasant place, painted in bright colors, where four women and one man cared for eighteen children. There was a great deal of one-to-one contact between the adults and children. Joyce was well known to everyone and immediately became caught up in the activity; the whole effect was of alive, aware, warmly interacting people, children and adults. One report has estimated that home-bound mothers and their preschool children spend on the average of fifteen to twenty minutes a day in meaningful interaction.[14] Joyce's solution to child care seems infinitely preferable.

Day care and nursery school may also be important for girls in helping them to achieve a sense of the possibilities of their own bodies. Increasingly, day care is providing a setting in which girls can experiment with a number of different kinds of competency, including traditionally masculine activities such as using hammers and nails, or playing with cars and trucks. One day-care center reports that the influence of live models is particularly strong. After observing a woman construction engineer at work, for instance, some girls began using blocks to build structures for the first time.[15] One mother, a carpenter, built a climber for her daughter's nursery school, where the girls have received special encouragement to go outside and climb. But mothers of children at another day-care center said ruefully that the center had attempted to encourage both boys and girls to play with dolls and trucks; left to themselves, however, each sex gravitated to its traditional toys.

In the preschool years the influence of cultural stereotypes, as presented by television, books, and often by grandmothers and other relatives, seems to be as strong as the example of active, working mothers—perhaps stronger, in view of the nearly universal appeal of dresses to three- to five-year-old girls, no matter what the life style of their mothers.

Daughters like Sally are definitely aware of work as part of their mothers' lives, yet nursing remains as popular a career goal for preschool girls as it ever was, even when, as with one child, an aunt is a doctor! But underneath these stereotypes, daughters are dealing with messages that are more important—the messages they are getting from mothers about personal and sexual identity. If a mother feels good about herself and is able to communicate to her daughter that she feels good about *her*, the more superficial aspects of role identity will not be so crucial, a point we will be referring to throughout this book.

Many mothers feel quite bemused by their daughters' attraction to dresses but feel the best thing to do is to let them wear them if they want to, partly on the theory that refusal or discouragement will only produce a rebellious reaction. Kate said, "Ann loves getting dressed up for parties, and she likes to wear pink a lot. I hate pink but I indulge it because I don't want her to have a terrible reaction to my tastes."

Kate perhaps summed up the feelings of many mothers about attempting to counteract cultural stereotypes. She said that a lot of parents she knows have talked to their daughters about gender roles, but she feels that if she talked to her daughter, Ann would either not really understand or would want to do exactly the opposite. Ann's favorite story is one with a feminist slant, in which the heroine, instead of marrying the hero, goes off by herself to discover new cities. "But she always says at the end, 'I think she should have married him.' So she's getting a lot of things that I can't do anything about. I think a lot of it comes from TV. I think the best thing I can do is to be an example."

On the other hand, Yvonne has weeded out her daughter's books and will sometimes point out, during a television program or when her daughter is playing, that cultural stereotypes are not necessarily the only way to be, that she herself lives in a different way. Only the future will show what effect such attempts at counteracting role stereotypes will have. Children from three to five are engaged in figuring out the great questions of sexual differentiation and identity, and stereotypes undoubtedly have great appeal to them because they simplify matters: girls wear dresses, boys don't; I am a girl, therefore I want to wear a dress. Later on, more subtle differentiations may be possible, but only if they are offered as real possibilities.

Little girls who want to be nurses are probably responding to the image of nursing as a concrete activity involving close personal care of patients, a mothering function. They are at an age when they are extremely interested in mothering, and it is possible that nurses are close to their present image of reality. Only when cultural images of women are sufficiently wide-ranging to offer more choices will it really be possible to tell how much little girls' perceptions and ideals are merely received images and how much they are chosen to relate to the real world of four-year-old fantasies and preoccupations. In the meantime, helping girls to develop competency in nontraditional areas such as hammering nails, climbing, and standing up for themselves is not likely to make them less female—although it might alter our stereotypes of femininity.

III

BODY AND THE SEPARATE SELF

There is the body. A daughter lives in it and with it, and she must find out what it means to have her particular body, with a vagina, without a penis. As we saw in the first two chapters, a daughter's response to her body as an instrument for exploring the world and as the medium through which she gains her first sense of herself as a separate and competent person is profoundly affected by her mother's response to her earliest behavior. In this chapter we will explore some of the ways in which sexual identity is affected in much the same way.

I have suggested that personal identity, gender roles, and sexual identity can be usefully explored as separate aspects of what finally becomes a daughter's complete sense of herself. In Chapter II we found that it is peculiarly possible for girls to identify themselves as girls without at the same time having a clear sense of being separate persons. Perhaps it is more difficult to separate gender identity and sexual identity, because at the deepest level they are related to each other in ways that aren't always very clear. On its most basic level, of course, gender goes beyond roles; it says simply, "I am a girl." Gender roles, then, mean, "This is how I should behave to show that I am a girl," or, "When I behave this

44

way I feel like a girl." Sexual identity says, at first, "This is how I feel about my body," and, later, "This is how I feel about my body and my sexuality in relation to myself, to other women, and to men."

As a child grows, all these aspects of identity overlap. Margaret Mahler suggests that the process of separation and individuation is largely completed by the age of three.[1] By then a child usually also has a clear sense of gender: she knows that she's a girl. But the process of gaining a clear sense of sexual differentiation—the Oedipal period, in psychoanalytic terms—goes on until five or six. A daughter's growing sense of her sexual identity depends at least partly on the extent to which she is able to feel that she owns her own body and experiences it as part of herself. Perhaps only then can a girl go on to gain a clear sense of her body as specifically female, as opposed to male, which is what the process of sexual differentiation is all about.

Gender roles may help in consolidating a daughter's sense of identification with her mother, but mothers who have a vague or negative sense of their own sexual identity will pass on their feelings to their daughters, no matter how clearly defined gender roles are. If a mother has not been able to grow to personal and sexual maturity, if she has a stake in keeping her daughter infantile and dependent, she will not enable her daughter to achieve a sense of her own sexual identity. She may even emphasize the more superficial aspects of gender roles because of her own conflicts or insecurity about herself and her sexual identity.

At the same time, a developing sense of sexual identity is part of a developing sense of self; and security in these aspects of identity may make gender roles simply less important. As one sixteen-year-old girl put it, "If you know you are a woman, you can do anything and it will express your femininity, because that's rooted in your sexuality."

The social climate in which girls discover what kind of value is placed on their being girls, as opposed to being boys, will strongly affect their sense of their sexual identity.

Perhaps the most important aspects of this social climate are created by a girl's mother. It is in the context of her relationship with her mother that a daughter will learn whether she is free to explore and enjoy the potential of her own body. From her mother she will get her first cues as to how she should feel about her sexuality, cues that may become clear only when she has matured.

At about eighteen months, a child begins to be toilet-trained, to be able to feed herself, and to be increasingly conscious of her own body and of differences between the sexes. The way her mother handles these phases of development will have a profound effect on a daughter's perception of herself and her body.

Erik Erikson has described toilet-training and physical exploration (both exploration of the body and exploration of the world with the body) as stages in which a child develops either autonomy and initiative or a sense of shame and guilt.[2] We have already seen that traditionally girls have not been encouraged to develop a sense of autonomy in exploring the world with their bodies. It is possible that early toilet-training is one of the subtle ways in which a sense of shame, a sense that she is not in control of her own functions, has been imposed on little girls. Until Dr. Spock came along in 1945, toilet-training was considered best done as early and as quickly as possible, and many parents continue to believe this. It is not uncommon for mothers to try to toilet-train an infant of six months. The burden of this kind of thinking may fall more heavily on girls than on boys, for girls are proverbially easier to train than boys. Their greater physical coordination may contribute to this, but it is also true that neatness, cleanliness, and self-control are more likely to be expected of daughters than of sons, as was shown so clearly in John Money's case of the little boy who was reassigned as a girl.

Yvonne recalled, "My mother told me I was toilet-trained at twelve months. I remember, although this must have been

later, being put into underpants and told I would be spanked
if I soiled them. My revenge was to wet my bed at night, but
that used to make me feel terribly ashamed because I felt I
couldn't control myself."

Rigid feeding schedules for babies were also common
until 1945 or 1950. Under such a regime a baby might be
expected to eat when she was not hungry, or was too exhausted from crying to want food any longer.

Toilet-training and feeding herself are activities a child
learns to do slowly. She is making a transition from being fed
and from impulsively relieving herself to performing these
activities autonomously and in a controlled way, in specific
places, and at more regular times. If her mother expects a
"good performance" too early, before she has the necessary
muscular coordination, she will not have a chance to learn
that she can be in control of her own body. She may end up
performing merely to please her mother. If her mother does
not allow her autonomy when she is ready for it, she may be
forced to continue relying on her mother long past the point
at which she should be able to take care of herself.

Kate told me, "I was force-fed until I was ten. My mother
fed me with a spoon until I was seven or eight, and then I
would be told I couldn't do this or that until the food was
finished. There was always more food than I could handle so
I was always throwing up."

But girls are not alone in being subjected to inappropriate
toilet-training or forced feeding. Why, then, should these
"invasions" have more severe consequences for them than for
their brothers? The answer lies in the word "invasion." Erik
Erikson has found that very early on little girls develop a
sense of their own inner space—of the openness of the vagina and the receptive nature of the womb. Open spaces are
vulnerable, which may make little girls particularly sensitive
to any form of invasion of their bodies.[3]

Rigid toilet-training, arbitrary feeding schedules, and
forced feeding are ways in which a daughter learns that she
does not own her body: her mother remains in command.

This makes it all the more difficult for a daughter to recognize that she is separate from her mother, and to learn to enjoy her body and take pride in her ability to master its functions.

It is a commonplace in psychoanalytic literature to find that disturbances in the early mother–daughter relationship are related to later disturbances in or confusion about sexual identity, which for a daughter must include a sense of her relationship to her vagina. Later fears of the vagina as an entrance into the body may have their origin in infancy and early childhood, when the little girl learned that she had no control over what went into or came out of her body.

Another way in which damage is done is through a kind of mystification of the female body. Too often a daughter's attempts to clarify her sense of her body and to experience its possibilities for pleasure are frustrated by her mother. Ellen vividly recalls her mother's response to her masturbating and to her earliest questions about sex:

"I remember that when I started asking questions about sex, when I was four or five, she would be very vague, and I could sense that the questions disturbed her. I remember being very worried about just how you got to have a baby. I was afraid that something just happened to you, you had no control over it, and I was afraid it might happen to me. So I asked her how you knew when you were going to have a baby, and she said, 'Oh, you just know.' That didn't help me at all; I went on feeling that something might just happen to me at any moment. The other feeling I got was that I had upset her a lot just by asking the question.

"I don't remember when I started masturbating, but I remember when she found out about it, and how upset she was. I was about six; she was giving me a bath, and I was rubbing myself, and she asked me why I was doing that. I didn't know how to tell her I was doing it because it felt good, so I said, 'It itches.' She told me that it was very bad if it itched there, it might mean that there was something wrong with me. She really scared me. I grew up thinking that if I masturbated it meant there was something wrong with me; I was afraid of my own body."

The traditional repression of women's sexuality results in further damage to a girl's sense of physical autonomy and pleasure in her body. Mothers who communicate anxiety about specific sexual questions and react with disapproval toward masturbation are not likely to help a girl develop a positive feeling about her own sexuality. A daughter may know she is a girl, but she won't learn to feel at home in and with her body. Again there will be the sense that her body is not under her own control, that it is somehow "foreign territory," and therefore frightening.

Kinsey suggested that more small girls may masturbate to orgasm than small boys, partly because of girls' greater physical coordination.[4] But the evidence suggests that if they don't have a secure feeling about their bodies, such an experience can be quite frightening, which of course may have repercussions later on.

Joyce described her reaction to discovering orgasm as a child: "I remember having an orgasm when I was quite small, perhaps about four or five. I was sitting in front of a mirror, and I must have been touching myself. I didn't know what it was. I remember being absolutely overwhelmed, and not knowing what had happened. I think the idea of trying to do it again might have been frightening; it was something that happened and then went away.

"The impression my mother gave me—and my friends feel they were given the same impression—was that sex was something you discovered when you started going out with boys. It was something waiting for you out there.

"I didn't consciously start masturbating until I was 22, and then I realized what had happened when I was a child. It was a very strange experience, like losing myself, or going completely outside myself. As a child I couldn't handle it. It has taken me a long time to feel comfortable with my body. Feminism helped—the idea that masturbation wasn't terrible, and the discovery that I wasn't alone in not knowing what my body was all about. I finally discovered that sex was something I could enjoy, and that it is really attached to my body and relates to my needs."

Not all the mothers and daughters I spoke to have grown up with such a sense of mystification about their bodies, of course, but such experiences seem more common than not. One exception I met was a seventy-five-year-old grandmother who talked to me quite frankly about her own and her daughter's sex education: "Mother was a devout Catholic, but fifty years ago she was already advocating the reforms of the sixties. She believed in a great deal of personal freedom, and she was in favor of birth control. She said that in a big family the mother was worn out and couldn't give her children the attention they should have. She was very careful that my sister and I were thoroughly instructed about sex, which was simply not done at that time."

"It wasn't done in my time, either," I said.

"My daughter said the same thing. When she was in college, she told me that she and a group of friends had been discussing how they learned about sex. Out of the whole group she was the only one who had specific sex instruction from her family. I can't believe it! How could you possibly leave children open to so much trauma? I guess I started on my daughter when she was almost an infant, by pointing out how dogs are shaped differently from each other and letting her watch when the females had puppies. Certainly by the time she was seven or eight she had a pretty good idea of sexual relations."

Many new mothers today feel very strongly about enabling their daughters to be at home with their bodies. A greater awareness of the importance of physical autonomy has changed the climate in which children are toilet-trained. Now that the child's developmental processes are understood, the gradual learning of control is emphasized. Nevertheless, the old ways die hard. Joyce told me, "Before feminism, we were all defensive about our images as mothers; we worried about things like how early our daughters were toilet-trained. Boys were supposed to make mistakes, and be more impulsive, harder to train, but it was different with a daughter. By talking with other mothers at the day-care center, I found out that some children weren't trained until they were three or three-and-a-half. It gave me more confidence to let Carol work it out at her own pace."

Masturbation isn't as upsetting as it once was either. Kate expressed a very common attitude when she talked about the climate she is trying to provide for Ann's early sexual explorations:

"I think she was born open and free; I think we were all born that way. I enjoy touching her, and looking at her, and she enjoys herself. When she asks me about her vagina, I always mention sex along with bearing children. I don't want her to limit her idea of her body to bearing children. I say that it feels good to touch your clitoris and she says, 'Oh, it's wonderful, I love it, and it tickles.' I always bring a little pleasure into it, whenever that's brought up. I like my body now, but I don't think I always did. I think that part of growing up with my mother was that you weren't supposed to acknowledge that you were a sexual person. It's so exciting that Ann feels free with her body, and enjoys it.

"Until recently she used to masturbate fairly casually in the middle of doing something else, like eating dinner or playing. I can't imagine that I would have been allowed to do that as a child. I have absolutely no memory of masturbating until I was about eleven or twelve, and I discovered it all by myself. But Ann always amuses me, and I've never said anything. She seems very matter-of-fact about adult nudity, but lately she's become more shy and guarded and sort of coy about her own body; she doesn't want anyone to see her nude, especially men, although it doesn't bother her if I'm walking around without any clothes on."

Still, a relaxed attitude about their daughters' sexuality doesn't always come easily, no matter how much mothers may desire it. When you can't recall masturbating until you were eleven or even nineteen or twenty-five, when as a little girl you had no idea you had a vagina or clitoris (or, if you discovered them, the knowledge was repressed), there are bound to be some internal repercussions when your daughter asks questions. It is inevitable that young mothers will continue to have some doubts about how they respond to their daughters' questions and feelings about sexuality, and even that they unwittingly pass on double messages to them. Yvonne recalled, "My mother was very enlightened in some ways, and she explained the process of reproduction to me, but we could never talk about sexuality. I would like Vicki to be up front about her own sexuality."

Yet, Yvonne put Vicki in an uncomfortable situation even as I was talking to them. She had told me that she didn't like Vicki to use "gutter language," such as "doing pussy," but while we were talking she asked Vicki if she could describe "doing pussy." Vicki clammed up. She confided to Yvonne that she was afraid because I was there, which seemed quite reasonable, but it also seemed clear that Yvonne was overanxious about the whole issue. There was obvious confusion between Yvonne's use of a phrase she condemned and her desire for her daughter to be able to discuss sex with a stranger, as though it were a subject like food or school. Yvonne seemed to be repeating her own mother's double message.

A woman's feelings about her body probably can't be separated from her feelings about men, and the way she sees the vagina and penis. She may fear sexual intercourse as a psychological invasion, an invasion of her whole self. She may even confuse the physical events of sexual intercourse with her feelings about sex roles, seeing males as irretrievably brutal because, as one angry lesbian declared at a workshop on sex roles, "They fuck women." "Fucking" then becomes synonymous with "fucking over"—with simply using women.

If we see ourselves and the world originally in terms of

our bodies, a controlling, invading mother, who does not allow her daughter to develop a secure sense of her separate body and separate self, can permanently damage her daughter's sense of herself as a person and as a sexual being. Unfortunately, the tradition that has emphasized a negative attitude toward the sexuality of girls and women has insured that this kind of damage is passed along from mothers to daughters. The purpose of this tradition may have been to insure that female sexuality was held in abeyance until it could be channeled into the socially required roles of wife and mother, but it has had the disastrous consequence of preventing women from developing a clear sense of their personal and sexual identity—which has in turn perhaps made them more dependent on a constricted gender role for their sense of identity.

Freud was very aware of the effects of extreme sexual repression on his male patients; he saw that it led to intellectual timidity and a lack of self-assertion. But because he, like the society of his day, equated femininity with the virtual absence of sexuality, these qualities in girls and women were simply taken as part of the definition of normal femininity.[5] They were ascribed to biologically caused problems of development, in the course of which girls had to give up a "masculine" sexuality and arrive at "feminine" sexuality through a difficult path of development that left them passive and, it seemed, too exhausted for any real development as persons. It remained for later psychoanalysts, such as Karen Horney and Clara Thompson, and sex researchers, such as Masters and Johnson, to assert that sexuality is just as "feminine" for girls and women as it is "masculine" for boys and men.[6]

The idea that a daughter's relationship with her mother underlies her later relationships with men is not a new one. In his 1931 essay "Female Sexuality" Freud wrote, "We see then that the phase of exclusive attachment to the mother . . . is far more important in women than it can claim to be for men. . . . Many a woman who takes her father as the model

for her choice of a husband . . . repeats with her husband her
bad relations with her mother. . . . The mother-relation was
the original one, upon which the father-relation was built
up."[7]

It is interesting that both Kate and Yvonne, who described
their mothers as possessive and invading, had the same feelings about their relationships with men. Kate described her
feelings very clearly: "I have always been invaded by the
men I know. The price I paid for their company was dependency and having limited space for myself. I have never
known a man who didn't take bits and pieces out of me."
Kate, and several other women, experienced this feeling
mainly in terms of gender roles, which have traditionally
encouraged women's dependency on men. But it seems clear
that the foundations for sexual, as well as gender, identity
are laid down in early childhood, in the context of the relationship with the mother, and that being able to value and
possess our bodies is related to our ability to value ourselves
as persons in the world, which of course affects the way we
relate to men.

The psychoanalyst Edith Jacobson has pointed out that
until about the age of three, it is common for daughters to
have fantasies about merging completely with their mothers.[8] They have not yet learned the difference between de-
siring someone and identifying with her. Freud saw that a
daughter's first love-object is her mother, and that her problem is to shift her attachment to the father. In the essay just
quoted, he made several important observations. He said
that a little girl's desire for an exclusive attachment to her
mother may last into her fourth or fifth year and that during
this period she sees her father as something of a rival for her
mother's love. Only gradually does she shift her focus to her
father. However, Freud speculated that many women never
really abandon their original attachment to their mothers.

In a sense, then, all little girls are "homosexual." Some psychoanalysts theorize that when the mother is ambivalent
about her own sexual identity, the daughter is unable to

break away and develop heterosexual interests of her own.[9] Lynn Carson chose to "come out" as a lesbian after several years of marriage and two children; her memory would appear to confirm this view. "I knew quite early in life, before I really knew what it meant, that my mother's sexual relationship with my father was not satisfying to her. She found sex very disturbing, and she found her own body disturbing. At the same time, she needed and loved me much more than I was willing to accept. I had this emotional intimacy with her that I didn't really understand."

Lynn said that despite the fact that she had been married, she felt as though she had remained a child until she came out at twenty-seven; I asked her whether that meant that she hadn't really felt like a separate person.

"No, I didn't. I didn't make any decisions about what I was supposed to do or be. I accepted all the conventional images. There was, for me, a sense of power in coming out— I was making a statement about my life."

Whatever combination of predilection and circumstances combine to incline a woman toward homosexuality, its roots appear to be in what Dr. Marjorie Taggart White expressed as "an undying fidelity to the mother."[10]

Dr. Barbara Sang, a clinical psychologist, pointed out to me, however, that there are many different kinds of psychological configurations that can be called lesbian; a woman who has never felt herself to be attracted to men at all will have a point of view different from Lynn's. And Edith Jacobson suggests that homosexuals can have a strong sense of self; it is their concept of their own or their mother's sexual identity that differs from a heterosexual woman's.[11]

As a little girl, Ellen was also very attached to her mother, but remembers that her mother was rather erratic in her expressions of affection. However, Ellen's parents appear to have enjoyed their sex life. "I remember being intensely jealous of my father when he came back from the war. My mother belonged to *me*, and he was coming between us. It's funny—I remember my mother being very distant from me most of the time, but at other times she would suddenly scoop me up and hold me close and hug me and kiss me. I remember always wanting more attention from her, but those moments were frightening. I felt as though I couldn't breathe —it was suffocating.

"I had been sleeping in my mother's bedroom, and I guess they didn't move me out right away when my father came back. I remember seeing him with an erection, and I saw that he could be close to her and I felt she cared more about him than she did about me. I thought his penis was like shit he could keep, while my mother threw mine away. And I thought it was like a club, too, it looked like a club he was holding in front of him, and he might do me in with it. I thought he hated me and was as jealous of me as I was of him. All I wanted was to keep my mother with me, because without her there seemed so little of me. But he got in the way."

Ellen's memory is a good illustration of the way small girls organize their thoughts around their own preoccupations; toilet-training can be a battle for autonomy in which a child's feces represent part of her body that she wants to keep, or at least keep control over. In Ellen's fantasy, her father could hang onto his feces, which became both a weapon and a way to get closer to her mother. On one level, Ellen identified strongly with her father as the possessor of a penis; this gave her the opportunity to be someone unlike her mother, and so escape "suffocating," while at the same time she could keep her mother. On another level, however, she projected her anger at her mother and her father onto her father, which made him seem very frightening to her; his penis became like a club.

As Clara Thompson suggested, "The penis as a symbol of aggression stands for the freedom to be, to force one's way, to get what one wants. These are the characteristics which a woman envies in a man. When this envy is carried to a more pathological degree the woman thinks of the man as hostile to her and the penis becomes symbolically a weapon which he uses against her."[12] Recall the lesbian for whom "fucking" became "fucking over."

Any little girl might have feelings and fantasies of this kind, but Ellen's were aggravated by the fact that her mother was both very distant and, at times, disturbingly close. Ellen felt that there was very little of herself.

For most people the process of growing up seems inexorably to involve accepting the fact that they belong to one sex or the other and that there are limitations on their future sexual possibilities. Very small children seem ready to fantasize the social and biological characteristics of both sexes; only slowly, through the gradual realization and acceptance of who owns what sexual equipment and—if only on an unconscious level—of what John Money calls "the reproductive and erotic roles of the sexes" do they come to accept their own particular sexual identity.[13] For a daughter, the ease of this realization may depend to a great extent on how much support she gets from her mother for her evolving sense of her femaleness. If her mother enjoys and takes pride in her own sexuality, if she feels fairly secure in her relationships with men, she can be supportive toward her daughter.

Six months ago Sally asked her mother the classic question: where was her mother's penis? Ellen told her she didn't have one.

"You *never* had one?"

"No."

"Will I have one?"

"No."

"What do I have?"

"You have a vagina," her mother told her.

"Oh."

Sally already knew she had a vagina. Ellen recalls that as early as one she had discovered it, and by two was sometimes putting candies or other small objects into it. But now the fact has taken on added significance because Sally is engaged in working out the difference between the sexes and, ultimately, her own sexual identity. It is no longer simply a question of her own body, but a question of how there can be two different sexes, and how they relate. And despite the fact that her mother is a successful career woman, and has always been open and frank with Sally about sexual questions, telling her what her vagina was as soon as she asked, Sally is still going through some confusion about who possesses what physical equipment. No doubt Ellen's continued openness will help Sally work her way through this question successfully. But the question remains. It is part of the process of separating from her mother, and the fact that she feels free enough to ask such questions suggests that the separation is occurring successfully.

As Freud saw it, when a little girl realizes that she does not have a penis, and so cannot ever really possess her mother, she becomes angry at her, blaming her for not giving her one of these magical organs. It is partly this anger that leads her to turn away from her mother and take her father as the object of her love.

Mildred Moskowitz, Director of the Borough Hall Office of the Madeline Borg Child Guidance Institute of the Jewish Board of Guardians, told me that usually by two-and-a-half a daughter in a two-parent family begins relating differently to her parents, becoming seductive toward the father. The rivalry and competition with the mother become part of the process of separating from her, while the father provides a balance in mother–daughter hostilities. Joyce's experience with Carol is a good example of this. She recalls that "when Carol was about two-and-a-half she became very affectionate toward my husband, and at the same time didn't want me to do anything for her, or even with her. It was all her father. I felt jealous, and a bit guilty. I thought she was rejecting me because I was doing something wrong. Naturally, because she was in day care, I immediately assumed it was because she was spending too much time away from me. Finally I realized that she was just going through a process of growing up, and I stopped trying to compete for her attention. Lately, we've become friends again."

A daughter's love of her father and anger toward her mother during this Oedipal period are not absolute. As a daughter separates from her mother and competes with her for the love of her father, she is also identifying with her as a female. Again, this is partly dependent on how much support she receives from a mother who has a clear sense of her own sexual identity and values her own and her daughter's femaleness. This in turn will enable a daughter to develop a sense of herself as a whole person.

Clara Thompson wrote, "I believe that much more important than penis envy in the psychology of women is her reaction to the underevaluation of her own organs. I think we can concede that the acceptance of one's body and all its functions is a basic need in the establishment of self-respect and self-esteem."[14]

But if a mother's relationship to her own sexuality is negative, vague, or ambivalent, she is less likely to be able to support her daughter's development of a sexual identity. A mother may feel trapped in an unsatisfactory role relationship with a man. She may overidentify with her daughter's Oedipal conflict, replaying through her daughter her own unresolved conflicts of sexual identity. In such a situation, she may not be able to allow her daughter to take this step of separating from her. As Edith Jacobson points out, although it is normal for a small daughter to have fantasies about merging with her mother, her mother has to know that she is separate from her daughter in order to encourage the child to separate from her.[15]

Yvonne recalls, "My mother was very bosomy, and I remember I used to love to snuggle up to her. We had an almost incestuous, lesbian kind of thing going on. She'd rub my neck, and I'd play with her hair; it was very sensual. And she indulged it, like it was okay to do that, since it was two women.

"But I never learned anything about my own body; I never realized I had a hole. I didn't know that pubic hair was hair; I don't know what I thought it was. I don't have any conscious memories of masturbating as a child. And as I got older, I began to realize that my mother was very upset about my sexuality. I began to have the feeling that her femaleness was very phony. She didn't really like being a woman, and certainly not sexually. I have finally come to the conclusion that she is afraid of men. I don't remember ever seeing her being affectionate with my father, and since he died she has not let a man touch her."

When Yvonne did eventually marry, she did so, as she expressed it, mainly to please her mother, and, like many other separated women I spoke to, felt her sexual relationship with her husband was something less than satisfactory. She now lives alone with Vicki, finding in her work and in her ability to cope successfully with her life a sense of autonomy that may be the beginning of a real sense of separation from her mother. In a childhood context in which she was not encouraged to experience her body as separate from her mother's, she evolved a kind of pseudoheterosexuality, as, indeed, she felt was the example given by her mother. The fact that she still refers to her vagina as a "hole" is an indication both of Yvonne's immature sexual development and of the sense of vulnerability that has prevented her from learning to enjoy her own sexuality.

The effects of maternal seductiveness on sons have been widely explored, and it is generally accepted that a mother who has an unsatisfactory relationship with a man will tend to be seductive toward her son, with serious consequences for his developing sense of sexual identity. But the effect of maternal seductiveness on daughters has been less widely considered, perhaps in part because women's sexuality has been invisible unless seen in relationship to men. But it is precisely this fact that may contribute to the intensity of some mother–daughter relationships. If it is only men who come between mothers and daughters, rather than a mutual acknowledgment of their separate identities as persons, then covertly they become interchangeable, fused personalities, with no means of distinguishing themselves from each other except insofar as they relate to men. This can lead to confusion of sexual and personal identity with gender roles, so that for many women a rejection of traditional gender roles leads to insecurity about sexual identity, and insecure sexual and personal identity will lead to a flight into rigid gender roles. Lynn recalled, "I had to learn the role; the whole business of femininity was an overlay. My mother learned and followed the same rules and it was an overlay for her too. She passed on to me her own sense of conflict between the qualities demanded in her job and feminine qualities, and she certainly passed on her conflicts about her sexuality."

This is not to suggest that fathers are of no importance in a daughter's developing sense of sexual identity. But in identifying with her mother, a daughter is going to take many cues from her mother's sense of herself in relating to the world and to men.

In the traditional nuclear family, in which a mother stays home, part of a father's function has been to provide a "bridge" to the outside world. His presence and his daughter's attachment to him help her break away from the close tie with her mother. But, in Mrs. Moskowitz's view, a working mother can provide the same bridge to the outside world.

Separated mothers do have the problem of what to do about lovers, whether to let them sleep over or to try to keep them apart from the mother–daughter relationship. Yvonne decided to stop having her lover sleep in the house because she feels she is not likely to marry him. If Vicki forms an attachment to him, and he eventually disappears, it will be one more loss for Vicki to bear. But at the same time, Yvonne is concerned about the absence of a father-figure in Vicki's life: "The only thing I wonder about is, what kind of vision is she getting of me because there is no man around here? So there I am, bringing her up in a world without a man, and I wonder about that. I don't think it's good for her."

In Mrs. Moskowitz's opinion, a home without a father does not necessarily create an unhealthy situation for a daughter. If a mother is getting support for herself through work, friends, a lover, or an extended family situation, she can handle and even encourage her daughter's separation. In addition, she points out, a stable environment can make up for emotional difficulties, and a father in the home who is not providing real emotional support for a mother can have a negative effect on both mother and daughter.

What about the increasing number of single mothers who are raising daughters alone? Or any mother who is worried about where to draw the line between openness toward her daughter's sexuality and too seductive a relationship? Kate expressed her conflicts about this: "I'm always touching Ann, as an expression of love, and she's very physical. It worried me for a long time, especially the fact that she wanted to touch back, and I thought, my God, she's homosexual. From the time that she could go into the shower with me I became conscious of the fact that all she wanted to do was touch my breasts, and look at my body, and that this was exciting to her. I let her do it, because I was brought up in this almost Victorian atmosphere, where you don't even have ankles. I didn't want her to feel that the grownup female body is some kind of mystical place, separate from where she's going, or negative. But at some point I do withdraw, and she must sense that, because she withdraws, and then the whole thing becomes easier for me. But I'm never sure what I'm conveying when I say 'no.' "

Probably the only answer to this question is to determine where the mother's real energies are going. If she is able to find satisfaction in areas other than her relationship with her daughter, she is less likely to be seductive or possessive to the point of confusing her daughter. The fact that Kate does "turn off" at a certain point suggests a healthy attitude. By saying "no" she is conveying to Ann the boundary between exploration and erotic over-involvement.

IV

WHAT ARE LITTLE GIRLS MADE OF? SOME ROLES AND REALITIES

More and more women are changing the focus of their lives to include work as well as home. The mothers we met in Chapter II are trying to change some of the traditional ways of relating to their young daughters by encouraging autonomy and independence at an early age. By changing their own lives, they are also offering their daughters a new definition of femininity; they want to give their daughters the chance to identify with them as strong, achieving women as well as mothers.

Bridging the gulf that has developed in our society between home and work is not easy, however, and ideas of appropriately feminine or masculine behavior change very slowly. Mothers must sort out the messages they received from their own mothers about femininity, and they must also deal with a social definition of femininity that is still being expanded to include self-assertion and achievement. And so, increasingly, must their daughters.

As girls move into the world of school and the larger society, they are faced with contradictory expectations. On the

one hand, they are encouraged to do well in school; on the
other hand, their achievement has little to do with their
future place in the world.

Their "real" education is taking place on another level. In
their textbooks and on television they see women who conform to the traditional image of wives and mothers. At home,
they usually help their mothers with cooking, cleaning,
sewing, and even mothering if they take care of younger
brothers or sisters. Traditionally these domestic roles for
girls have been the ones that point toward the future of
adult realities, in which their identity as women will depend
more on their success as wives and mothers than on any
achievements of their own.

At the same time, preadolescent girls are allowed more
freedom from gender roles than at any other time in their
lives. They are often allowed to be tomboys—to ride bikes,
climb trees, play baseball or even football. But to be a tomboy is to behave "like a boy," to indulge in fantasy. Preadolescent boys, on the other hand, are learning the value of
competency, mastery, and achievement, which they will be
expected to put into practice. They are learning the rules of
the game of manhood. Womanhood is a different game.

One reason why girls are allowed relatively more freedom
in preadolescence, and another reason why their freedom is
illusory and contradictory, is that they are not considered to
be sexual beings—they are not yet capable of bearing children. After puberty girls traditionally have been set apart,
no longer permitted the freedom to "play" at masculine roles.

In fact, girls at this age are quite interested in exploring
sexuality; "latency" is beginning to be understood as a term
that merely describes the fact that preadolescent children
have not yet experienced the resurgence of hormonal activity that comes with puberty. Elementary school girls are
learning social attitudes toward sexuality just as they are
absorbing social attitudes toward other aspects of their identity. Unfortunately, the "public" image of sex they receive

from other children too often suggests that it is something forbidden and "dirty." As discussed in previous chapters, mothers can reinforce this attitude by their disapproval of their daughters' explorations, a disapproval that is bound to help alienate a daughter from her own body.

Ellen told me, "I remember that from about six on my friends and I were absolutely consumed by sexual curiosity. Once when I was eight or nine a girl friend and I were discovered by her mother at the innocent occupation of trying to discover whether we had grown any pubic hairs. Her mother told mine and we were both punished. My mother was so angry I was really frightened. There was such a split; we were all—boys and girls—playing sex games and showing each other our genitals and so forth, but we were all aware that it was essential that our mothers never find out."

If the major emphasis is on a daughter's being neat and clean, a mother can tell her daughter about sex in such a way as to reinforce the street attitude that sex is dirty. Eileen Johnson, who was raised on a farm in South Carolina, has done this with her daughter Lacey. "Clean" means according to God's plan, because Mrs. Johnson is deeply religious.

"Lacey will ask, 'How does a baby get inside your stomach?' I explain that this is God's plan; marriage is a sacred thing, because the Bible tells you you should get married. When you do, there is a seed from the man and one from the woman, but God is the one who multiplies it. As long as she knows it's God's plan, she won't think of it as filthy. She has heard a neighbor and me discussing our pregnancies, and the troubles my neighbor had, and how far along I was when I had the caeserian for Lacey, but we never discussed it in a real dirty way. I've told her that when she gets older, kids are going to tell her dirty ways, but she don't have to believe them."

This combination of matter-of-factness and an underlying emphasis on pain and "filth" is at best providing Lacey with a fairly negative view of female sexuality. It is calculated to reinforce the morality of sex only within marriage, while suggesting that sex for pleasure, as opposed to reproduction, is dirty and should be denied.

But if a mother is relaxed about sexuality and able to communicate easily with her daughter on the subject, then this is a particularly important time to begin counteracting stereotypes and childish fantasies and emphasizing the positive aspects of lovemaking.

Virginia Freeman remembers one scene from her daughter's preadolescence particularly vividly: "Amy had asked me questions about sex since she was very small, and I had answered them. She seemed very relaxed about it. When she was nine, she found my birth-control pills, and asked, 'Are these birth-control pills?' I said, 'Yes.' And she said, with some fear I thought, 'Do you and Daddy want another baby?' I said, 'No.' She asked why I took them, and I said so we could make love without having a baby. She burst into tears; I was completely taken aback. Nothing had led me to expect her to be shocked. Then she said, 'All the kids in my class think it's dirty and I guess I've been infected.' She sobbed in my arms for an hour. Kids in her school had told her you didn't do 'that' unless you were going to have a baby. Some of them thought their parents went to a doctor's office; the general opinion was that sex was dirty."

Amy, who is now sixteen, added, "I think I got most of my information about sex from my mother, although I heard a lot on the street, such as that the man pisses inside the woman. I wasn't disgusted by it; I thought, 'If that's the way it's done, it's okay; Mommy says it's good, so it can't be that bad.' "

Learning about social attitudes toward sexuality is only one aspect of the immense learning process that occurs in preadolescence. Girls are absorbing the whole range of social attitudes toward their gender, and are discovering what kinds of behavior are expected of them in terms of their futures as women. In middle-class homes, these messages have become increasingly conflicted, as the dichotomy between home and work has become more clearly defined. In working-class homes, this dichotomy is still largely resolved by seeing work as, simply, work rather than a career. Working-class mothers may work, but their main orientation continues to be domestic.

Eileen Johnson recalled, "My mother had seven children. She didn't have time to really love us up; I remember it was hard to go up to her and kiss her because she was constantly busy with cooking, washing, canning. There was no such thing as women working in those days. My parents were good to us; we never felt unwanted, but I never remember my mother kissing us goodnight."

Eileen now lives in a small town in West Virginia, where her husband works for a lumberyard. She has two older sons and her daughter, Lacey, who is ten. Eileen works in a local factory to supplement her husband's income, but her main concern for her daughter is that she grow up to be a good wife and mother. She is proud of her daughter's housekeeping abilities.

"My sisters and I always helped in the house. If we didn't do it right my mother never hollered at us. She would say, 'Now let me show you how you really do it.' Like sweeping with a broom; she taught us to keep the dust together. And I teach Lacey that way. When I work the third shift, I tell her not to wake me up until noon, because I come in at 7 A.M. I tell her to watch TV and stay in the house, and then I get up and make her lunch. And the house looks as if I'd straightened it myself. She washes the dishes. My mother would say, 'Make sure you wash that dish properly. Don't give it one swipe.' So I showed Lacey, and I'd put her up against any adult washing dishes. And when she takes her clothes off, she always folds them and puts them right back in the drawer where they're supposed to be. I never have to touch her room except to run a sweeper and dust."

Eileen takes her housekeeping seriously; it is the core of her identity, and she is passing that message on to Lacey.

For her mother, raising seven children and doing the cooking, washing, and canning was surely a full-time job and in another age would have been considered real work—women's work, but no less real than men's work. It is a measure of how much our concept of work has changed that Eileen Johnson can say, "There was no such thing as women working in those days." The work Mrs. Johnson's mother raised her for was real, but it has been made largely obsolete by technology and an emphasis on smaller families. Yet women are still expected to define themselves through woman's work. Like many women, Mrs. Johnson has begun to realize that her priorities are shifting. But, also like many women, she is training Lacey for the old role.

"When I was young, I wanted to stay home; I cleaned over and over. To be in the house meant everything to me. Then, when I got older, I didn't care about cleaning that much. I used to wash my windows once a week; now I wash them once a year. It's funny; I had started my change of life. I was very nervous and had hot flashes. I began yelling at Lacey a lot.

"Then I went to work. I hadn't had a period in over a year; I worked two weeks and got a period. I was so relaxed, because I was getting bored around the house. My work is really tedious, but I enjoy it. I have a big machine, I set the dials and test the parts they make. My mind is occupied, and I have enough energy for a twenty-five-year-old. And every month I get my period. I believe it's because I'm so relaxed."

Lacey herself has chosen to be a "good girl." But she is an active child, something of a tomboy in fact; and there is a suggestion of future ambivalence and possible rebellion in her feelings about growing up: "I'm a tomboy. I do what boys do. Some girls don't like snakes, and I do. Most girls don't like to play baseball; they like to sit around and play with dolls. I like baseball and football."

"How do you feel about growing up?" I asked.

"It comes. You don't have much choice."

"How do you think you might feel when it comes?"

"That I'm old enough to take care of myself, go out and work for myself, have my own living. "

Yet she wants to get married and have "one boy and one girl, so my boy can go out with my husband hunting and the girl can stay home with me."

Contradictions between home and work are expressed, but not in a way that suggests they are consciously perceived as opposing roles. Eileen would like Lacey to live nearby when she gets married: "I tell her to be a good wife. If she has to work, I would like to take care of her children, while her and her husband are getting ahead, so it wouldn't be as hard on her as it was on me."

To Lacey and her mother, as to many working-class women, work is not a career; a woman's fundamental occupation remains motherhood and housework. Whether Lacey will be able to continue this means of integrating what for many middle-class women have become two different roles remains to be seen.

Roles are important at this age, and although girls are increasingly exposed to influences from the outside world, their mothers remain the central figures in their lives, for in their mothers' lives daughters see their own futures.

Susan Anspach was raised in a middle-class urban household. She told me how conflicted she felt about her mother when she was a child. On the one hand, her mother insisted there was only one path Susan could expect to follow if she was to be a contented woman; on the other hand, Susan could see the harsh realities of her mother's life that might be her own one day.

"My mother stayed home all the time, but she wasn't very happy with what she was doing. I don't know how many women would describe their mothers as happy with what they were doing, but I think mine was particularly unhappy. The whole message was that if you were an unselfish person you got married and had children, and that was very fulfilling. On the other hand, she was very unhappy, very unfulfilled. She wasn't happy doing the things she was telling me would make me happy. She never admitted her predicament.

"The whole thing about my mother was that there just wasn't much to identify with. All the time I was growing up, the only interesting people in my life were men. Everything that was exciting or interesting was male. I think my mother was particularly uninteresting.

"When I was seven I started reading all the time, I guess as an escape. I wanted to grow up to be a writer, but I could never see beyond that; I don't think I ever saw a future as a woman. The message I was constantly getting was that if you were a woman and thought of yourself as something else besides a wife and mother, there was something very aggressive, selfish, and nasty about you.

"During the war, my mother took me to a female pediatrician. Every time we went she made a special point of telling me that all the men were away in the army, and that was why we had to go to a woman doctor.

"At the same time, I had a maiden aunt who went to college; she was held up to me as someone who thought she was smarter than all the boys, and look what happened to her. It would happen to me if I got too educated. I should never act smart around a boy. The funny thing was, my maiden aunt never seemed to be so unhappy. But she was held up to me as an example of how terrible it was to live alone, to fail to get married and have children.

"I still have trouble with feeling that if you're a woman and you want something more than a family for yourself, there is something wrong with you."

Susan is expressing one of the most common predicaments of the daughters of Mom—that their mothers' role and that of women in general offered no way into the future with which they could identify, except negatively. To begin to think seriously in terms of achieving, or of playing an "unfeminine" role, was to identify with a "masculine" role.

Unless a daughter is very lucky, and receives support and assurance from her mother that roles labeled "masculine" by society will not compromise her developing sense of herself as a woman, she may split her sense of self into 'masculine' and "feminine," and this can produce serious problems. A strong sense of self depends very much on a sense of continuity between the options available for the future and the knowledge that in realizing these options one is or is not realizing one's full potential. The sense of self is still developing in preadolescence. Sexual identity and gender roles become part of it, and when there are serious discontinuities between a girl's sense of herself and her own potential, and the people she is encouraged to identify with, there are bound to be repercussions. As the psychoanalyst Edith Jacobson suggests, a daughter's developing sense of personal identity will be strongly affected by her sense of her future role in society.[1]

Most achieving women continue to be what feminists call "male-identified." They feel, as Susan did, that men and men's activities point toward a future they can accept. But this presents problems in terms of a girl's growing sense of herself. If her sense of a woman's role, of her future identity as a woman, is negative, the ground is laid for an overidentification with men, either through choosing a masculine role, often at great cost to herself, or through choosing a feminine role and identifying less directly—but no less disastrously—with the interests of her husband. In the latter case, she is very likely to grow up to repeat with her own daughter the contradiction between overt message and covert reality that Susan's mother presented to her.

Susan now feels that her mother, in holding her maiden aunt up as an example, was perhaps covertly suggesting that there was an alternative to the role of wife and mother. But it was presented as an either-or situation—a double bind in which whatever Susan chose, she would have to lose. If she chose to follow the path of personal achievement, she would never be loved as a woman and would have a lonely life. If she chose to follow her mother's example of a traditionally feminine life, she was liable to be as miserable as she felt her

mother to be. This is the essence of the double message that
has traditionally been given to women in our society: if you
achieve, you stand alone; if you choose not to stand alone,
you give up yourself. No wonder Susan saw no future as a
woman!

In passing along a double message to Susan her mother
was, of course, expressing her own sense of conflict about the
double message in her life, and the option she had chosen.
She was not able to be as consciously aware of the conflict as
Susan is, but the feeling was there. This sense of conflict
about roles has been growing in women for some time, as the
range of activity allowed women has narrowed through the
development of the modern family and the removal of productive, economically necessary work from the home.

In preindustrial Western society, home and work were not
as separate as they are today. In *Housewife* Ann Oakley
points out that before industrialization the home was likely
also to be a workshop in which husband, wife, and appren-
tics shared work, child care, and domestic chores. Boys
and girls were apprenticed out at an early age, and women
themselves might work independently of their husbands. In
fourteenth-century England they were listed as "brewers,
bakers, . . . , and workers of wool," and through the seventeenth century married women who worked had the same
legal status as men.[2] In America, of course, the tradition of
pioneer women who could plow and shoot as well as raise
children continued well into the nineteenth century.

But with the development of industry, productive work
became more and more concentrated outside of the home.
As Philippe Ariès shows in *Centuries of Childhood*, the idea
of the home as we know it—a place separate from the world,
where a woman lives and takes care of children, and to
which a husband returns at night from the world of work—is
quite a recent development in modern history.[3] As an ideal,
"home and family" grew up with the industrial revolution.
Today, of course, woman's work has all but disappeared;
women can choose between the kind of compulsive house-

keeping Eileen Johnson recalls herself doing or moving out of the home in one way or another.

As the scope of woman's work dwindled, the fashion of an idle wife developed among the middle classes, and continues today; it is the mark of a successful man that his wife does not need to work, and many women have grown up absorbing that ideal. At the same time, the idea of childhood as a separate stage of life evolved. In the Middle Ages, as Ariès shows, children were regarded as miniature adults; the evolution of the modern family included the evolution of the concept of childhood and of the importance of child care. Primary responsibility for this care fell, of course, to women.

Partly as a result of these trends, an elaborate rationale for 'gender roles' evolved in modern thought, according to which "normal" femininity became tied not so much to the realities of woman's work, but to an ideal in which women live emotional, 'expressive' lives with and through their husbands and children, while men live individual, 'instrumental' lives. Men do, women are. This ideal was implicit in the development of the modern family, which depended on the submergence of women's social identities in those of their husbands and, increasingly, in those of their children.

Achievement, or the serious, self-identifying pursuit of one's own interests in the world, became masculine. Loving dependency on your husband and the raising of his children, with vicarious involvement in your husband's interests and your children's lives, became feminine. In the preindustrial West, a woman might very well become involved in her husband's work, but her involvement was real, not vicarious. She did his work with him or for him while he was off fighting or whaling. Imagine a modern executive's wife actually carrying on his work while he goes off to an international sales conference!

Gradually, then, femininity came to embody more an absence of self than the possession of it. Personhood became legally and socially embodied in men. Elizabeth Janeway expressed her sense of this development in her book *Man's*

World, Woman's Place: "If they are normal women, they are
abnormal people; if they are normal people, they are abnormal women."[4]

This is the message a daughter begins receiving from society at an early age, and that many daughters like Susan
receive from their mothers as well. A vision of a future in
which she is expected to live through others is, at best, likely
to produce a rather vague sense of self. If a daughter is
unable to see into the future in terms of wider roles than
motherhood and domesticity, her sense of self will begin to
be constricted before it has fully developed, because she will
see that in adulthood she will be expected to give up a large
part of whatever personal autonomy she does develop.

Paradoxically, as the actual range of productive activity
available to adult women became ever more narrow, girls
were allowed increasingly more freedom. As Ariès points out,
the idea of childhood for girls seems to have developed later
than it did for boys. Through the seventeenth century girls
were trained for their adult role as mistress of a household;
by ten they could do the work of an adult woman and by
twelve or fourteen they would be married. Depending on
their class, they might also be expected to learn a trade;
lower-class girls might even learn to write. Running a household might involve management of production and income
from poultry-raising or other activities. There was thus little
discontinuity in women's lives; expectation and opportunity
were continuous from childhood to adulthood. Given this
continuity, and given also the wider range of economically
functional activity included in woman's role, a positive sense
of female identity might actually have been easier to develop and maintain than it is today. The childhood training
and adult roles of women were solidly grounded in socially
and economically functional activities.

The evolution of modern society has changed continuity
into discontinuity. Girls today are allowed nearly the same
freedom as their brothers, while their adult lives are in many
ways more constricted than were the lives of women in the

past. Preadolescent daughters may choose to be tomboys as a sign of rebellion against this sense of a constricted future; they are rejecting those aspects of femininity that include passivity and dependency as well as the more superficial standards of dress or behavior codes.

Ellen found that when she compared her mother's role with her father's she experienced an identification conflict that she has only gradually been able to resolve: "I think I really wanted to be a boy at that period. I wanted to be separate from her, I wanted to be on my brother's and father's side. I tried so hard. They had these codes, like, 'You don't cry when you get hurt.' When I was six I had a wart taken off my thumb. It was cut out with a knife, with no anesthesia, and I didn't cry. I kept sitting there saying, 'tears don't come, tears don't come.' My father said he was proud of me; I was a real marine. And my brother was really impressed.

"My mother wasn't taken seriously by either of them, and I wanted to impress them that I was just as tough as they were, that I wasn't some sort of laughingstock, as they seemed to think my mother was.

"Yet at the same time there were lots of things I loved about her; she had a really good sense of humor, while my father was always very gruff. And she loved to take off and do things at the drop of a hat. I liked the exotic things about her too. I remember them going out at night. My mother would come in looking fantastic, and wearing some incredible perfume, I thought she was a movie star or something. When I got a little older I wanted to be like a better version of her, so I would be taken seriously."

Another woman recalled the strong effect on her of once being mistaken for a boy:

"I was a rather fat little girl and lousy at sports, so the idea of being a tomboy never occurred to me, although I envied the girls at school who were. When I was around ten I lost some weight, was told I didn't have to wear glasses all the time, cut off my braids and cropped my hair short. I remember the day I had my hair cut. I was out shopping with my mother and, although I was wearing a skirt, the woman behind the counter couldn't see it, and she called me "son." I felt this tremendous surge of power and pride. I looked at my mother and thought, poor thing, no one would ever mistake *her* for a man. I started walking with big, jaunty strides until the girls at school made fun of me."

Along with industrialization, education has of course contributed to the conflict in women's lives between public, masculine roles and private, feminine ones. While education for girls did not really become common in Europe until the nineteenth century,[5] a rudimentary education was provided in America from the time of the earliest colonies. But as the educational opportunities for girls extended from reading and writing to high school and then college, the real goals of women's lives did not significantly change until educated women began to demand changes, a process that is still going on. Mothers of all classes are still primarily concerned about their daughters' futures as wives and mothers. A girl's education may be a sign of status to her parents, or it may be seen as a necessary preparation for acquiring an educated husband. Only rarely do girls grow up with the expectation that their education is preparing them for the future pursuit of some goal of their own.

At the same time, however, they are expected to do well in school. It is well documented that girls do better in school than boys; they consistently get higher marks, particularly in reading and writing. But again, this achievement does not point toward the future. Girls who get higher grades than boys in high school are less ambitious in their career plans, thinking in terms of becoming secretaries or nurses rather than executives or doctors. By college, girls seem to demonstrate a real fear of success, because success contradicts everything that is expected of them as women.[6]

"I had just turned twenty when I got married," said Mary O'Reilly, who is now thirty-seven. "My sister got married at sixteen. I worked for the electric company for six or seven years; I quit after my second child. My grandmother had taken care of the first one. She more or less brought her up."

I asked her about her twelve-year-old daughter's education.

"She's very bright. When she was small she was like an old lady rattling on. She could really sit down and hold a conversation with you. When she was in kindergarten they wanted me to put her in a special school, where they have courses for very bright kids; I said no and sent her to parochial school."

"Would you want her to go to college?"

"If she wanted to go; that would be up to her. I feel this way: college is no good for girls. You figure, they're going to get married and they're going to want kids. That's going to be the education thrown right out the window. Like me: I quit working when I had the kids. How can you work when you've got to raise kids? It's impossible."

For Mary O'Reilly, achievement in school is a good thing now, and she is proud of her daughter. But present achievement has no bearing on future plans. Her daughter wants to go to a business high school and then perhaps work as a secretary until she gets married. She doesn't see any conflict between being bright and being a woman, because the possibility of using her intelligence in any nontraditional way simply hasn't occurred to her. She lives in a family and culture that are still relatively solid and continuous in their expectations for women. Her family probably would be considered lower-middle class, but they remain very close to working-class ideals, buttressed by Irish Catholic traditions.

Whether Mary O'Reilly's daughter remains unconflicted as she grows up remains to be seen. In another household the conflicts are already out in the open. Betty Giles is forty-five and lives in a fashionable east coast suburb. She is worried about her daughter's present goals and about how she will adjust to adult life.

Claire is eleven, and she has two goals in life: to be a genius and to ride on the U.S. equestrian team. In pursuit of her second goal, she is currently taking riding lessons. In pursuit of her first, she wants to get straight A's in school, although her mother, an easygoing woman, claims to put no particular pressure on her. Claire told me she was upset because she got one B on her last report card. Betty told me, "We don't want a genius, we want a mentally stable child." "Mom, I want to be a genius," declared Claire. "I don't want an overintelligent female who won't be happy later on in life," Betty told her. She said to me, in front of Claire, "She's been tested very high in IQ. I don't think very bright girls necessarily have more problems than most girls, but I want her to be happy no matter what life brings. A very, very intelligent woman might not be happy with a home, and I don't want this for her, as an only child. I would like her to have a good marriage with a family of her own later on. Really intelligent women aren't happy with certain normal things of life. Certain things will keep me happy; I can take a little course, take skating lessons, work with the PTA. Claire never held me back. Not that I'm at my happiest doing this, but it fills the void for now. And I would like to see her happy in life, as an individual, as a squared-off adult."

Claire at this point announced that she doesn't want to get married; she thinks it is hard to be married and have a career. "Mothers should be around most of the time, but mine has been around long enough. You can do what you want now, Mom."

"What if she wants to pursue a career exclusively?" I asked Betty.

"Fine, if that will make her happy. If that will make you happy, honey, you can do anything you want in life."

The double message here is right out in the open. Claire's pragmatic awareness of the choices offered by society is new; it is awareness on a conscious level that was not available to Betty's generation, or to Susan's. There is no way of knowing what kind of solutions Claire will choose, but at least she seems to know what some of the options are. It is possible that Betty's outspoken ambivalence has helped Claire. Betty herself feels she married rather late; she worked for fifteen years as an executive secretary and was happy to quit; she refers to her job as 'exposure.' "I very much wanted a child. I did my thing; I was more than willing to give it up. In another seven years I'll be ready to go back."

"Do you think there is an inherent conflict between having a career and a family?" I asked.

"I'm finding it among my friends. They've had their families, and now, because of the messages they're getting from feminism, they've become martyrs because they haven't got careers. I feel sorry for them."

Of course, the problem is that most women still don't want to have to make an absolute choice between marriage and motherhood on the one hand and a career, or at least work, on the other hand. The mothers we saw in Chapter II are trying to reconcile these two poles, using day care or a housekeeper as the bridge. Most of the preadolescent daughters I spoke to suggested, as Claire did, that they preferred having their mothers available to them. Girls of this age are consolidating their identities and need very much to feel loved and supported by their mothers. "Availability" is a tricky word; a mother can be physically present and yet not be emotionally available for support. Women who believe in day care reason that it is better for them to be really available when they are with their daughters than simply to be physically present all the time. But a demanding career can create a situation in which a mother most often is not there, either physically or emotionally. Mildred Moskowitz, of the Jewish Board of Guardians, cited the example of the nine-year-old daughter of a successful professional woman who asked her mother whether her work was more important than she, her daughter, was. Her mother answered that work and a child are not the same thing. But such a distinction is hard for a daughter to make; Mrs. Moskowitz suggests that a

child needs to know she is the most important thing to a
mother.

If husbands really help in taking care of children, they can
provide a measure of emotional availability. A housekeeper
can provide this too, but, as Mrs. Moskowitz pointed out,
she can't replace a mother unless she becomes, in effect, the
mother herself. And this is a problem because housekeepers
leave, or mothers get jealous and ask them to leave.

Most of the women I talked to had jobs that gave them
a certain degree of flexibility—teaching, writing, or some
kind of free-lance work that allowed them to spend time at
home. Several mothers spoke of taking their daughters with
them when they went out on free-lance assignments or to
conferences as consultants or editors. Amy Freeman recalled,
"For a long time my mother worked in the house, so she
was still there when I was having problems at school. I
could always go home during lunchtime to talk to her, and
explain stuff to her, and cry. I feel proud of her working
now, but I don't think I realized it then. I thought everybody's mother worked; I didn't know very many kids whose
mothers were housewives, so it wasn't a big thing. I think
she was concerned about the effect of her working on us, and
I think she realized that it wouldn't be the same as being
home all the time. That might be a little better for the kids,
but only on a short-term basis, because in the long run she
would feel unhappy, and that would reflect back on us, so it
wouldn't have done anybody any good if she had stayed
home. I don't think I felt neglected."

Her mother, Virginia, took up the story. "In my day, being
a feminist meant that you worked, but you were still supposed to be the top mom. I don't think my relationship with
my daughter would have been as good if I hadn't worked. I
had a marvelous housekeeper who gave the kids a lot. I
would have been awful if I had been with them all day,
because I can't stand that kind of life—you are ghettoized. I
didn't think I was capable of spending my whole day at
home with little kids; and you're not really with them; you

have to shop, and so on. I also think it was better for them to have some other influence on them besides me."

Virginia Freeman somehow pulled off the difficult feat of being both top mom and a career woman. But other women, even mothers, feel they have to make a choice. Those who choose the masculine side of the double message may feel that they have failed to live up to the feminine ideal, that they aren't top mom, and they may take it out on their daughters because they feel guilty and because they expect too much of their daughters and of themselves. A successful executive, whose daughter attempted suicide during a "sophomore slump" in college, talked to me about her daughter's childhood:

"There is something that goes on with women that is very serious. I see it in literature, in *The Bell Jar*: women who are educated and have a certain assertiveness if not given the chance to use it, subconsciously do use it against their sons or daughters. I was using it, for myself, but I think there was also the backlash that comes from not getting the social acceptance that one should. I was kind of walking two streets, and taking out my guilt at what I was doing on my daughter. Like my mother, I was overcritical. I think my daughter found it impossible to really please me, or I didn't expect to be pleased by her.

"I think we want *things* for our daughters instead of wanting them to be happy, instead of spending the time to really see what their needs are and to be available to them. What is really important is being able to help them get that sense of building themselves, block by block, so they know who and what they are and what they want to do with their lives, whether it is to be a housewife or a doctor. This is the role we are supposed to play as parents. But we're busy asking for social acceptance for ourselves. Even though working women are rebelling against society, we are still within its confines. I think the people who have been successful with their children have examined who they are and what they want for themselves and opened a dialog with their children, so that the child can say, 'Gee, Mom, I like you when you go out and do all of these things, and I like the time you spend with me, and right now I need a little extra time.' I think I wanted this kind of open communication, but I didn't know how to begin it. In a way I was expecting my daughter to demand it of me—but she didn't have the ability to demand it of anybody, not even herself."

In short, a mother must reconcile both personal and social demands, which often are confusing and contradictory, as they were for her mother, as they may be for her daughter if the mother has been unable to deal with the discontinuities in her own life.

Work may not be the only thing that takes a mother away from her daughter. In fulfilling a traditionally feminine role she can be equally unavailable. Many upper-middle-class daughters remember their mothers with great bitterness. Caroline Lavalle has two daughters of her own, both of them approaching adolescence. She grew up in an upper-middle-class southern household, where she was attended mainly by a maid.

"My mother was very elegant and very beautiful, always out in the evenings. I remember one time when I went to the market with her; she had to go because the people didn't deliver. Hell, that was once! To go to the market with your mother. She was very elegant, very much up in the clouds, and very put out by having me. She didn't know it, but I think she really would have liked to have been a lawyer. As a child I heard over and over how bright my mother was, and how marvelous; it seemed to me that she had made some horrible mistake when I was born.

"I grew up not wanting to be a girl. It never occurred to me that I wouldn't be a boy. I would ask the maid, 'When am I going to be a boy?' She would say, 'Sweetie, you kiss your elbow and you turn into a boy.' I would have broken my arm."

Caroline's mother had become a distant image, so distant and glamorous that Caroline could never live up to it. Her fantasy of becoming a boy seemed the only way to resolve her conflict about the impossibility of ever becoming like her mother.

There are, then, two important ways in which mothers can influence their preadolescent daughters' development. One is by serving as a role model that a daughter may perceive as desirable or undesirable. The second, and probably more important one, is the extent to which a mother makes herself available to her daughter. Roles in the abstract mean little to a daughter who simply wants her mother's concerned attention. A mother who feels conflict about her role—whether because, like Susan's mother, she chose a traditionally feminine solution to the double message or because like the successful executive, she chose the masculine solution but feels guilty about it—is not likely to provide the kind of attention and support that a daughter needs. If a mother feels herself to be a whole, adult woman, and is able to be supportive, she can help her daughter weather and even resolve the double message society still gives. She can support a daughter who wants to be a tomboy without implying that the girl is endangering her future as a woman. She can do this even if she herself has chosen a more traditional role. One study of the lives of successful women executives found that although their mothers represented the traditional feminine role model, they also actively supported their daughters' total freedom of exploration of what were considered male roles.[7]

Amy Freeman remembers, "When I was a little kid I was a tomboy. We had to wear dresses to school, and I'd rush home to get into my jeans to go out and play, and kids would say, 'is that a boy or a girl?' It made me feel terrible, because they knew I was a girl and they were just saying it to be nasty. It was my mother who helped me through it. She didn't try to stop me from being that way. She encouraged it. That was a strong stand for her to take, and it was important, because if she had tried to put a damper on that part of my personality, I probably would have been really messed up."

Virginia told me, "Amy was always warm and womanly, even as a tomboy. She always had a thing for children that I didn't have at all. I encouraged her to be athletic. My mother was terrible about femininity; she made my life miserable. I don't know why, because she was a professional woman herself. She had a master's degree, and she went back to teaching when she was older, after my father died. She wanted me to do things, but she really emphasized looks and femininity. The greatest goal was to get married, and raise a family; the other stuff was on the side."

Mrs. Freeman herself always worked, so she provided an example for her daughter that extended into the future. Perhaps Amy's tomboyish behavior was a way for Virginia to live out an old wish of her own: "I propagandized Amy that women should do things. She was always a tomboy, and I encouraged that because I thought it was healthy. I had never been a tomboy; I admired them but I was afraid to be one."

However, it is not essential for a daughter to become a tomboy as a means of separating from her mother, or as a prelude to achievement in later life. If personal and sexual identity are fairly secure, it is possible that roles can take their place as merely roles: activities or ways of behaving that express different parts of a girl's personality but that do not represent her entire sense of identity.

The Martinsons are an extraordinary family. I talked at length with the mother, the eleven-year-old daughter, and the grandmother, and I saw how an integrated sense of identity can be passed down from one generation to the next. All three generations live under the same roof, although the grandmother, Alicia Blair, has her own apartment in the house. Ann Martinson now works full-time as a journalist; her daughter Karen goes to private school. In the material that follows, I will let each speak for herself. First, Ann:

"Karen is a neat companion; I love doing things with her. She has a rather subtle way of getting attention; she's a little manipulative. I had an aunt who said, 'She's the only two-year-old I know who is capable of having the vapors.' Once, when she was about six, we were in the Museum of Natural History and she was worn out; she sank to the floor with her hands on her head. We thought if we went around the corner she would follow, but she went to sleep on the floor. She has a very determined mind; she's not easily dissuaded. I've really encouraged her in this; I think it's an important thing for a female to have—not to be manipulative, but to stick to her guns, to know what she wants and say what she wants. I have tried to encourage her to say it, to come out with it rather than pout or be sad and martyred, which is a great tendency of all the ladies in our family, my mother included. I think you communicate that kind of thing to your children subliminally.

"I consciously try to make her understand that you mustn't let yourself be defined by the people around you, especially the men. The whole culture has asked women to define themselves by particular roles for so long that we have come to expect this of women. We expect little girls to serve, not little boys. I don't feel there is all that much difference between men and women, and I get upset by feminism in terms of its polarizing effect. It's doing just what it purports to be fighting. People are people; roles are often imposed.

"My oldest son is very bright and very verbal, and at first my daughter wouldn't compete with him in areas she thought of as his, like reading. Her IQ is as high as his, and their strong points are in the same areas. She loves babies and little children, but she feels that having more than two is irresponsible, and I tell her she is absolutely right—have two or only one. And she says, the question is what am I going to do with the rest of my life? I say, you can do anything you want to. You are so smart and beautiful and determined and organized, you can do anything. She is so exciting. I don't want to put terrible demands on her, but I feel her potential is enormous, and I say that to her a lot more than I do to the boys, because they're boys and the world expects them to do something, but it doesn't expect that of her, not yet.

"I didn't want to work while the children were little; I really enjoyed the first six years of doing nothing except relating to my husband and the children; then I went to work, at first part-time. I am a great believer in seasons. I knew I wanted to work, and when the time came to do so I would, because everybody had always told me I could. My mother was simply a mother and a wife; my father wanted her at home. I know that just before he died he had agreed that she could take a job, but I think if it had ever developed into a career, diverting attention from him, there would have been big trouble. But when I was a child, she never suggested that I wouldn't be able to do something because I was a girl.

"My grandmother was independent; she worked and raised a family on her own after her husband died, and Mother was independent in her own way. She would probably think a woman could do anything better than a man just because she's a woman. I did have great trouble being smart in school; I spent a lot of time at the end of grade school being torn up about being smart. I closed my eyes and went ahead and was smart anyway, and I felt alienated from the whole world. It was very painful. I wanted very badly to get all my children into a school where they wouldn't be penalized for being smart. They aren't at their school."

Alicia Blair remembers her life as Ann's mother: "My attitude toward children started with my mother. She always thought of us as persons; she never treated us like children. She expected us to be responsible, and I think I did that with Ann. It wasn't so much anything verbal, as an atmosphere I tried to create.

"When Ann was born I was pleased because I thought raising her would be fun. My mother lived with us. My husband and my mother never had any difficulty between them until Ann was born; then they each wanted to bring her up their way. But I knew what was going on, and had no compunction about saying, 'It's going to be my way.' I made Ann into more of a hobby than a child. Finally the three of us came to an agreement: we would each be responsible for one part of her upbringing and leave the others alone. My mother read to her, took her on walks, and told her stories—history was her field. I always wanted Ann to be herself, and to develop entirely along her own lines. But I was determined that if there were going to be mistakes made in bringing her up, they were going to be my mistakes. That was my only possessiveness. I had seen too many people interfering in other people's lives, people trying to keep peace at the expense of somebody else."

Eleven-year-old Karen had the good fortune to benefit from these independent women. I asked her what she thought a woman should do with her life. Her answer is an eloquent illustration of the fact that if a daughter is backed by a mother with a secure sense of her own identity, she will not need to fall back on stereotyped roles in order to establish her own place in the world.

"I enjoy being a girl; I think it's fun. If I were a boy with the nature I have now, I'd be a real sissy. I'm not very active; I play a little baseball and handball, but not all the time. Girls can do to boys what boys can't do to girls. Usually a girl will strike up a conversation, but boys will phone girls first; I'm not going to let that happen. I haven't started to go out with boys yet, but when I do, if the boy is shy with girls, I'll make the first move.

"Girls can definitely do as much as boys; there isn't anything a boy could do that some girl couldn't do. Some boys can do some things better than some girls, but on the average they can do the same things.

"I don't think getting married is important anymore. You used to have to get married to support yourself, but now you can get any job you want. I want to get married, it would be fun, but I'll wait until I'm around twenty-five or twenty-six.

"I think a woman should really do something with her life.

She might be perfectly happy with raising a couple of kids, but if she's very smart she shouldn't waste herself on just bringing up kids. She shouldn't work and leave the kids with a babysitter; she should get a job she can do at home. If you have young kids you shouldn't be an executive; after maybe fourth or fifth grade it would be okay.

"Some women don't know how to do anything because they haven't had the training; people don't expect women to be politicians or diplomats or ambassadors; they expect them to be anything up to a judge or a congressman. I think if you have an aptitude for it you should be trained for it, whoever you are.

"I see my mother a lot because she works at home; whenever I pass through where she's working, we talk. And we talk at dinner, and we've been known to talk for forty-five minutes at bedtime. But once in a while she can only kiss me goodnight and run downstairs. It kinds of bugs me that she always has to work; my father works just as hard. The one good part is that they both enjoy it.

"One thing I admire about my mother is that no matter how many tasks she takes on, she always finishes them, even if she's late."

Ann and Karen are lucky; they have had the benefit of relationships with their mothers in which the dominant tone was one of mutual respect and easy affection. Karen is developing her sense of identity in an atmosphere in which it is assumed that the contradictory social expectations of women can be resolved. There will be compromise, but no choice will be so absolute that it involves compromising a strong sense of self.

V

FRIENDS AND ENEMIES

Adolescence is a difficult time for both mothers and daughters. Daughters increasingly are feeling the pressure of an emerging sexuality that must be integrated with a developing adult identity. They begin to feel the full brunt of social pressure to be feminine: to be pretty and popular and to discount achievement as unfeminine. Their mothers may be giving them the same message: that the assertiveness they may have been free to express as children is no longer appropriate, and that although good marks in school still are desirable, they are not quite as desirable as preparing to attract the right sort of husband. If they are very lucky they will already have learned from strong mothers to pay more attention to their own realities than to the cultural imperatives with which they are bombarded.

To some extent a daughter's emerging sexuality is really a reemergence. The Oedipal conflicts discussed in Chapter III are revived, and mothers and daughters may become extremely competitive. As in the Oedipal phase, a girl's interest in men is a sign that she is separating from her mother. Adolescence, however, marks the beginning of a separation that eventually leads to the daughter's leaving home and her mother's sphere of influence. And, as in early childhood, the mother's own unresolved conflicts of identity may be revived as her daughter comes to terms with her own identity.

Much of a girl's attitude toward her emerging sexuality will already have been formed by her mother's responses to her childhood questions and sexual experimentation as well as by her own increasing perception, however unconscious, of her mother's comfort or discomfort with her own sexuality. Menstruation is a milestone in this process, a biological and psychological event affecting both a daughter and her mother. It marks the beginning of puberty, the dividing line between girlhood and adolescence. The way in which a mother has told her daughter about menstruation will affect her daughter's sense of this event as something to be feared or looked forward to. Her response to her daughter's first period will reflect the climate surrounding her own adolescence and is bound to have repercussions on the daughter's sense of sexual identity. If menstruation is a "curse," a cross to be born, a daughter may resent it as an invasion of her previously free body, and view it negatively. Her first period will become a source of alienation from her body rather than a sign of her developing womanhood, a welcome sign of maturity.

Some researchers, such as Natalie Shainess, have found that an astonishing number of mothers react negatively to their daughters' first period.[1] There is an old German custom in which, when a daughter tells her mother about her first period, her mother slaps her face. One woman I interviewed recalled this as a frightening moment.

Any daughter is bound to approach puberty with mixed feelings; one athletic eleven-year-old told me that she wasn't looking forward to her period because she liked her body the way it was; a few minutes later, she said she wished her breasts had started to develop because other girls she knew were ahead of her in this respect! But the feelings a daughter has about growing into womanhood, as represented by her mother, will influence the way her ambivalence is finally resolved.

Until relatively recently it was common for girls to grow into puberty with little or no information to help them understand what was happening to them. Knowledge was commonly gained from a mixture of myths and facts shared among friends. Open discussion about such an important event should be part of a whole context of ongoing communication between mothers and daughters that helps daughters to consolidate their identities as women.

Ellen Barbour, whom we met in Chapter II, recalls the kind of negative impressions she received: "I remember the day my mother told me about menstruating. I was in the fifth grade, and I had stayed home from school because I was sick. My mother was cooking brains. There was this awful stench that went through the whole house. She said, 'Come in here, I want to tell you something.' So we sat in the kitchen with the brains cooking away, and she said, 'Pretty soon now you'll be starting to bleed.' I didn't want to hear about it. Some friends of mine had already said something to me about it, but I didn't believe them. My mother was so uncomfortable, and it sounded so unpleasant, that I just didn't want to listen.

"When it finally happened, I was in sixth grade. I didn't tell her. She found some blood on my underwear, came in and said, 'I think you've started menstruating.' I said, 'It's none of your business.' But she brought me Kotex and a belt, and then she told my father. I was furious. She made such a big deal about it. On the other hand, I was also getting fairly big breasts and she wouldn't buy me a bra. She never could tell me anything about sex at all. I learned from a friend's mother.

"I didn't like getting my period at all; nobody had told me it would hurt, and that frightened me. I really thought I might bleed to death. Then I discovered that all my friends hated it too; we used to talk about 'falling off the roof,' and 'the curse.' "

This took place twenty-five years ago, but it appears that things haven't changed very much in some homes today. An eighteen-year-old who lives in rural New Hampshire told

me, "My pants were dirty, and I thought I didn't wipe myself, and then I went to bed and my whole bed was wet, and
I yelled, 'Mom, what's wrong with me?' She just said, 'It's
something that all women go through.' She handed me a
napkin and belt and said, 'Here, put it on.' I said, 'What's
that for?' I had no idea what it was until I had a course in
feminine hygiene in school."

The question of why menstruation has been such a thorny
subject for mothers and daughters is not easily answered. It
heralds the time when a daughter becomes defined by her
sexuality (that is, by her capacity to bear children), to
which most other aspects of her personal development
henceforth will be subordinated. Any mother who resents
the choices she has had to make is likely to react negatively
to her daughter's reaching this point. But social conventions
operate here too; until recently, it was simply not accepted
for mothers to acknowledge their own sexuality, much less
communicate fully with their daughters about it.

In the past, many mothers simply may not have known
how menstruation works, or understood its function beyond
the fact that once you start to menstruate you are old
enough to get pregnant. Claudia Nicholas recalls discovering her older sister's used Kotex and asking her mother about
it: "She was pretty matter-of-fact. She said that when a
woman reaches a certain age she bleeds, but it's nothing
bad. I don't know whether she even knew about the ovaries.
I didn't understand it. But I learned from my girl friends
that it was related to sex, and when it finally did happen I
remember feeling funny about my father. I felt proud, and
very much like a woman, but it was also awkward, with the
pad and so forth. I think the worst thing was just not knowing why I was bleeding. I plan to tell my daughter that it's a
good thing, the blood is there to nourish a baby and it is
washed out if there is no baby. You can tell kids a lot of
things that aren't terribly technical. I never knew that it had
to do with something good."

Claudia's first experience with menstruation wasn't entirely a negative one; despite a lack of information, her mother obviously had communicated to her good feelings about being a woman. This is a crucial factor. Ellen's and Claudia's mothers seem to have communicated about the same amount of information, but the way it was presented, the feelings and attitudes behind the information, made the experience of menstruation very different for them.

Yet one element was common to both: all they found out was that they would bleed. Nothing about the experience helped them to learn more about their bodies, to become more at home with their sexuality and so make it easier to integrate their sexual identity with other aspects of identity. Because Claudia's experience was more positive, she was less alienated, but she felt the same mystification about the body as Ellen did, a feeling passed on to them by their mothers. It's hard to feel that something that is mystifying belongs to you, and it's hard to see a mystery as being part of your identity.

As women's knowledge of their own bodies grows, they communicate more easily with their daughters about these matters; most of the adolescent girls I spoke to had been told what to expect by their mothers. Nevertheless, they still approached menstruation with mixed feelings, having absorbed the myths of society as well as their mothers' teachings.

A sixteen-year-old told me, "Mother had explained all about ovaries, and how I would begin to produce an egg every month, and how the blood was left over from getting ready for a baby. I knew it wasn't the kind of blood you get from a cut, but I still felt a bit scared about blood coming out of me. But I was wondering when it would start, and looking forward to it because it would mean I had turned a corner.

"I was thirteen. I was going to go riding. I went into my parents' bedroom—my mother was there alone—and said, 'I think I've just gotten my first period.' She said, 'What happened?' I said, 'I have little stains on my pajamas.' She looked at them and said, 'You're right.' 'Now I can't go riding today,' I said. But she told me of course I could. And that was it."

This girl's fear that she couldn't go riding when she had her period suggests that the old idea that girls become extremely vulnerable when they reach puberty lingers on. Until comparatively recently, it was thought that girls and women could somehow easily injure themselves while menstruating. This old wives' tale dies hard, the more so because it is related to the fact that menstruation makes it possible for a girl to become pregnant. As in Freud's day, puberty can still be a signal to a mother that it is time for her daughter's personal freedom to be curtailed. Self-assertion, when it is linked to a growing interest in boys, becomes dangerous, and a mother is responsible for keeping her daughter firmly in hand.

Mary O'Reilly remembers how her own attitude changed when Patricia reached puberty. "It started when she got her period. All of a sudden, when she said 'I'm going out,' I'd ask, 'Where are you going?' And I'd tell her, 'You can't go further than the corner store to get an ice cream.'

"The best thing a mother can tell her daughter is to be careful, right? I know a lot of kids, sixteen and seventeen, who got pregnant, and didn't even get married. The babies are orphans, and the girls are walking around doing the same thing all over again. I hope to God something like that never happens to us. I've known too many families who got hurt. But I know Patricia's friends, and she's good that way; I don't think she would get into any trouble."

If a daughter has been a tomboy, puberty is the time for her to give up her "boyishness." Her sexuality becomes "real;" it becomes the overriding factor in her life. She may have been competing in sports as aggressively as the boys she played with, and may have had considerable freedom to roam the neighborhood. But the older she gets, the more society expects her to conform to role expectations. The feminine role demands that she no longer compete with boys, but only with other women. Aggressiveness, or even self-assertion, is masculine, and no longer appropriate for her. Her battle for separation, for autonomy, must be kept within a narrow scope. However gently and easily control is applied, the renunciation of self-assertiveness and the independence to move about and explore her world at will is bound to affect her feelings about her own competence, about her ability to achieve seriously in the world. For boys, these links are, if anything, strengthened in adolescence; for any person, achievement as an adult inevitably depends on self-assertiveness and the ability to handle competitiveness. It is not strange, then, that girls come to value achievement less and less as they get older, and even begin to fear success.[2] Approval of them as women depends on giving up their assertiveness.

One mother summed up this problem as it affects her:

"I think I was always in conflict, but I wasn't aware of it until recently. I never understood that the messages my mother was giving me were aimed at me because I was a girl. When I began to work on my master's degree, my mother said, 'Why do you want another degree? You'll be smarter than all the men you know.' She was always thinking about marriage. Even when I was fourteen, any boy who came into the house was a potential husband. Her idea was that I should meet someone who would take care of me. And I did, but it didn't solve any problems for me; it didn't make me happy.

"With feminism, I began to realize that I have a terrible conflict between doing well and standing alone because of it. I was afraid to be better than men because then men wouldn't like me."

Marjorie Gordon and her husband live in a rambling house in suburban Connecticut, where they have raised five daughters. Three of the daughters are married and live nearby. Sylvia, who is now thirty, expressed how puberty affected her own life: "As a kid I was allowed a lot of freedom riding my bike and so forth, and I remember thinking when I got to be a teenager that all of a sudden my mother didn't trust me; that she took away my freedom."

"But I had other things to contend with," her mother interjected. "At thirteen you were giving parties, and we had to think about boys. It wasn't a matter of riding around on a bicycle anymore."

"It's funny, though," said Sylvia, "because I was pretty headstrong as an adolescent; we had a lot of problems. I was always rebelling for things like later hours. These days, with feminism, it's different, but when we were growing up we were taught that men ruled the world, so I always wanted to align myself with them because I was more aggressive than most girls. But when I became a teenager I started to think of myself as very quiet. I think the teenage years did that to me, some kind of insecurity that I still can't get rid of." Sylvia's childhood aggressiveness was "boyish"; when she became an adolescent her assertiveness became confined to a personal, domestic world, one she continues to inhabit.

A more open approach to sexuality hasn't necessarily made matters easier for mothers. The sexual revolution of the 1960s affected both mothers and daughters. Many daughters yielded to peer pressure to have sex at a relatively early age. It's not easy for mothers who were brought up to believe that you shouldn't make love until you are married to change their own attitudes when their daughters reach adolescence. For many mothers, the question of when daughters should start making love has shifted from "after she's married" to "when she is able to handle it." This is a more difficult standard to apply, and it demands more of the relationship between a mother and daughter than either the traditional standards or the alternative mode of abandoning responsibility altogether for the sake of permissiveness.

Sexuality must be combined with responsibility if it is not to become simply an arena for acting out hostilities between daughter and mother. The fact that some girls have sex and often become pregnant as a form of rebellion, or even as a way of looking for the love they don't experience at home has been well documented elsewhere. But for most mothers, dealing with their daughters' sexual maturation means balancing questions of responsibility and authority with concern for a daughter's welfare. Most mothers do feel responsible for their daughters, and they want them to experience their sexuality in a positive way.

Connie Maguire told me of her feelings about her thirteen-year-old, Christine: "The business of my being 'Mommy' really stands between us, and I would like to let go of that, to become less god and more human being. Sometimes my daughter and I can cut through it, but it isn't easy. And there are responsibilities I have. Up to a certain age, if she gets pregnant it's not her responsibility, it's mine—both emotionally and legally. There's a real limit to how much freedom you can give a daughter, when you know that if she goes too far it's going to come down on your head. You can brave the neighbors, but you can't be in contempt of court.

"And kids do a lot of acting out. If a girl gets pregnant, it's her way of confronting you with something. On the other hand, I'm leery of talking to her about contraceptives because I'm afraid everything I say carries such weight. If I offer to get her a contraceptive, it could seem that I'm saying, 'Why don't you get a contraceptive?' or worse, 'Why aren't you having sex?' I don't want her to feel that kind of pressure.

"Now she gets sex education in school, and that's a big relief to me. My mother had difficulty telling me about sex, and while I can talk about it, I'm not that comfortable with it. My daughter and I do discuss sex, but I'm afraid my own ambivalence may show. In school, it's discussed objectively."

Laura Harvey, who has a twelve-year-old daughter, Jennifer, described her attitude toward the question of sex education: "I want Jennifer to be aware of her own sexuality and to enjoy it. But not too freely. I'd be disturbed if she got involved in a homosexual relationship. I can't quite grab that whole bisexual business at all. It distresses me a great deal, in terms of my children.

"We talk about sex very freely, and she asks me lots of very sophisticated questions about things that never occurred to me until after I was married. We had a discussion about oral sex the other night. She touches on it and then goes off on something else. I don't push it.

"She's just beginning to be interested in boys, and I'm delighted. I'm terribly pleased that she is going to have breasts, because I didn't for so long. She's got more of a figure now than I ever had.

"I don't think I want her to have sexual intercourse until she can really evaluate it and appreciate it in terms of communicating with another human being, in terms of a celebration of herself. I think adolescence is too young to start, and I don't want sex to be diminished for her. By the time she's seventeen or eighteen she can start thinking about it, but I hope she won't when she's fourteen or fifteen."

Now that contraceptives have enabled adult women to dissociate sex from reproduction, mothers have become concerned about their daughters' developing sexuality as a means of finding pleasure and enjoying men on a more equal footing. But for adolescents, contraceptives remain problematical, even in relatively liberated circumstances. Jennifer told me, "I got the basics from my mother. We've got a science book that tells me anything else I want to know; there's not much I don't know now. You pick up a little from your friends, too. At least I know what some of the consequences are. Once I had a debate on abortion, so I did a lot of research.

"I think it's kind of dumb to have sex really young; you shouldn't start until you're sixteen or seventeen. I know what contraceptives are, and I think most of my friends do, but we don't really know how to get hold of them, or if we do, how they really work, like the diaphragm. And no contraceptive is foolproof. If you're fifteen and pregnant, it might ruin your whole life. You might not know what to do, or your parents might make you marry and you'd be divorced by the time you're twenty. I don't think my mother thinks I should have sex until I'm about twenty. I think you could wait that long if you want to, but not many people do."

Sixteen-year-old Amy Freeman, whom we met in Chapter IV, goes to a private high school in New York City. She said, "A lot of kids don't have sex for fear of getting pregnant. The pill and the IUD are dangerous, and the diaphragm is a pain in the ass. You might as well not have sex, or have it and not have intercourse; that's been the conclusion my friends and I reached. I don't feel any pressure to have sex; I think maybe five years ago kids felt a lot of pressure, but now nobody seems to care too much anymore. We talk about masturbating; my mother is still floored whenever I mention it. It's not an alternative, but it's one of the better ways to get to know your body. There's even some experimentation with bisexuality, but it's not publicly discussed. It's an option you could try if you wanted to."

Virginia Freeman remarked that Amy is very involved with feminism. "She's quite radical, and thinks her relationships with women are more rewarding than those with men. She thinks of men in terms of sex, and says masturbation is just as good. But she's very involved with her first real boyfriend right now and I wouldn't be surprised if she were about to sleep with him. I'm not sure how I feel about that. I feel a little uncomfortable thinking of her knowing I am a sexual person, so maybe it's not easy for me to think of her as having a real sex life."

It appears that contraceptives and greater sexual freedom have not meant that most mothers abandon their sense of responsibility for their daughters' well-being. They are now concerned about when and with whom their daughter will start making love. In a way, these questions make raising daughters more difficult, for the problems are seen in terms of individual development rather than in relation to settled convention.

Feminism has had a strong impact on many middle-class mothers and daughters, perhaps most noticeably during the daughter's adolescence. Adolescence points toward adulthood; mothers must come to terms with their feelings about letting their daughters go, and so must come to terms with their own lives. The conflict that often occurs in adolescence between mothers and daughters can be seen as part of the process of separation; daughters are beginning to assert their right to have separate selves and different values—to be independent people. Yet, at the same time, they still need their mothers in a number of ways. Sorting out their old dependencies from their developing sense of independence is a slow process. Mothers must begin to face giving up their daughters not only psychologically, as they did in early childhood, but literally.

Many mothers resolve this problem by wanting the same kind of lives for their daughters as they themselves led. By identifying with their daughters in this way, they don't have to give them up. Or, they may want a different kind of life for their daughters, and hope that through them they can vicariously experience what they could not achieve for themselves—a better marriage, a higher standard of living, or perhaps even the career they gave up because they had no support or opportunity to go beyond traditional roles. A mother who has been particularly frustrated in her identity as a woman may even want her daughter to live out the fantasies of rebellion or sexual freedom she never felt able to realize. It is a rare mother who has a good enough sense of herself and is sufficiently at peace with herself to attempt to deal with her daughter as another person, without at the same time abandoning her role as mother. For her daughter still needs her support, and, at times, her assertion of authority, based on her judgment as an older, more experienced human being.

In early adolescence, daughters commonly turn away from their mothers; it is a natural part of the separation process. At the same time, they seem to be looking for an ideal mother—one to whom they can talk in a way they no longer wish to talk to their mothers.[3] Many teenagers expressed this to me; they felt that a friend's mother was someone they could talk over their problems with, and that a particular friend had the kind of friend-to-friend, as opposed to mother–daughter, relationship that they would like to have with their own mothers. They feel that such a relationship is not possible with their own mothers because, as Connie said, mothers have such power and authority. In order to develop a sense of themselves, daughters must begin to break away from this authority figure, but they are not ready for independence, in any real sense of the word. So they are ambivalent. In the course of an interview with fourteen-year-old Lucy Miller, both sides of the coin were expressed. On the one hand, "Mothers and daughters should give advice to one another, and they do sometimes. A mother shouldn't just tell her daughter what to do; she should give her the information and let her daughter decide. But there are some strict parts to being a mother. You can't let your daughter be out all hours of the night; she might get hurt. A mother should be a mother."

On the other hand, "I've gotten more support from other people than I have from my mother. I really haven't wanted to talk to my mother; I talk to my girl friend's mother. I told my mother I couldn't talk to her because she was a mother; she wasn't a friend. Most of my friends' mothers are friends to their daughters." No doubt her friends feel the same way about their mothers.

The search for an ideal mother is part of the search for an ideal self, one who has already "arrived." It is a fantasy of a ready-made, grown-up self who no longer has to be a daughter to her mother, but can be a friend. Trying out an ideal self, or various ideal selves, is a way of reaching out toward adulthood, another way of separating. Only with separation is it possible to "return" to one's mother, to come to terms with the fact that growing up is a slow process, one in which a daughter has to learn that coming to terms with herself also means coming to terms with her mother and ultimately with her mother's imperfections and her own. In looking for ideal mothers elsewhere, and in trying to construct ideal selves, daughters are testing reality. By rejecting their mothers and idealizing other people's, they eventually will be able to reconcile themselves to reality.

Some form of adolescent rebellion has become an accepted convention in our society; yet, as Lucy Miller said, a mother should still be a mother. Insecure in their new ventures into independence, adolescent girls want lines to be drawn so that they can feel they have a secure base from which to separate.

Many mothers told me they feel that their daughters' rebellion is particularly intense precisely because the relationship is such a close one. Sons are usually less bound to their mothers, because they have shifted their identification to their fathers, and since fathers and sons usually see less of each other than mothers and daughters, this particular bond is less intense. Even when mothers work full-time, as increasing numbers are doing, the quality of subjective involvement, the intensity of identification between mother and daughter, is great. But separation may be somewhat easier for such mothers because their identities and energies are less bound up in their daughters.

A mother who had raised both a son and a daughter told me, "I think teenagers do want rules, but it's hard. And I would say it's harder with girls than with boys. I think girls are more fierce about getting their independence than boys, although they often don't really achieve it, in the end. But I think they're much more likely to rebel."

Ellen remembered a sense of real desperation about her own adolescent search for an ideal self, and her feeling toward her mother: "I think we all hate our mothers, although I think girls hate them for different reasons than boys. For girls, it has to do with identity."

"Do you think that girls hate their mothers as a way of asserting themselves as separate people?" I asked.

"Yes, I do. I couldn't stand to walk down the street with my mother. I had such a feeling of inevitability about it all; her lot was mine, and there was no escape."

"Daughters have to identify with their mothers, but they also have to differentiate themselves from them," I said. "I sometimes wonder if that's why women often seem to have more amorphous personalities than men do."

"Yes, they certainly do. Girls go through a whole process of adopting different identities."

"Don't boys do the same thing?"

"I suppose they do, but they don't seem to have the same sort of hollow sense inside, they don't seem to have the same kind of worry that maybe there isn't really anything there at all."

In Erik Erikson's terms, this feeling "that maybe there isn't anything there at all" would be explained by the fact that a woman possesses an "inner space"—she is literally "hollow inside."[4] But an extreme sense of having no self is not a normal condition for girls. It surely relates to a situation in which mothers and daughters are encouraged to be *too* close, to overidentify with each other, to be, in fact, interchangeable.

A mother sees in her maturing daughter the young woman she herself once was. This leads to competition, which eventually must end in the mother's realizing that she has to come to terms with her own aging. So there is a juxtaposition: the daughter is searching for an ideal self, while her mother must relinquish the sense of herself as a young woman, which may have become *her* ideal self, and which she is reluctant to abandon. The problem is complicated because, just as in early childhood, a mother is likely to find herself reliving her own youthful problems through her daughter. If she is going through menopause, which, like puberty, is a period of emotional and hormonal change that demands considerable readjustment of her image of herself, the problem is exacerbated.

Marjorie Gordon told me, "When your daughters get to the teenage years, and you're in your forties, you're going through an identity crisis too—'Who am I, and where am I going? What about me?' And you have to deal with their crisis as well. That's the hardest thing; you're hardly able to cope with your own emotional ups and downs, let alone theirs. You feel like a yo-yo; you have to do this for this person, and that for that person, and at the same time you're in inner turmoil. It's a very difficult time."

In the following dialog, a mother and daughter remember together how difficult communication became for them during these years. Ruth Sampson is now fifty; her daughter Shelley is eighteen. I talked to them together, and in the course of the interview they talked as much to each other as to me.

Shelley remembered, "Mother and I got along well until I was fourteen, when I stopped talking to her for a whole year."

"That's an extreme exaggeration," her mother put in.

"She talked to me, but I stopped talking to her. I was fat, and unhappy, and felt as though I was an outsider at school. I decided I was going to get 'in.' I was very calculating about it; I figured kids who are 'in' wear jeans, smoke cigarettes, go out with boys, go to parties, and take drugs. So I was going to do all of those things, but I messed it up. I had always liked dresses, and I bought the wrong kind of jeans, with seams down the middle instead of the sides. I would smoke in private but I couldn't bear to smoke at school, because I knew I was doing it just to be popular.

"My mother kept asking me if I really liked the other kids; I would say 'no.' Well, if you don't like them they're not worth it,' she would reply. It took a year for that to get to me. The horrible thing was that my mother was an ideal mother for a lot of my friends. They would tell me, 'She's perfect, you have nothing to complain about.' I would tell them they hadn't lived with her. I resented everyone thinking she was perfect, and that I had no right to complain.

"At the end of the year I had a party. I got all dressed up, there was wine, and I invited all these people who were older than I was."

"I was outlawed," said Ruth.

"To protect me so they wouldn't talk to her instead of to me," answered Shelley.

"The other thing that happened to end that period was that a boy who was known as this big stud invited me over to his house and tried to jump me. I decided that popularity wasn't worth it."

Ruth took up the story. "Shelley came home and told me he said, 'I've balled lots of girls on the first date.' She said to me, 'Mother, I have the feeling I want someone to make love to me, not to ball me.'

"Oddly enough I was never really worried about Shelley's losing her virginity prematurely; I've always had an enormous respect for her innate sense of balance. But I did spend sleepless nights worrying about her obvious unhappiness. I'd been through the same sort of thing, so I identified with her and probably lived through her troubles to an unhealthy degree. I had always had boys as friends, and then later I was the girl they would ask for help with their homework. But they didn't ask me out, and I remember sitting out dances in tears. I couldn't bear living through all that twice. And on top of everything else she was angry with me. Somehow it was my fault that she felt this way. Sometimes she would talk to me, and we would have a reconciliation, and that's when I would tell her that if she did something for herself, something that she enjoyed, it would belong to her and no one could take it from her. The other things would come in time. In our family we tend to mature somewhat later. We have little-girl bodies when friends have young women's bodies. I did, my mother did, my aunts did, my daughter did. I told her, 'Don't worry, we make up for it, we stay younger longer.' Which is also true; I'm still menstruating and I'm fifty."

"Now that I remember it," said Shelley, "it wasn't just that she was giving me advice, and it wasn't just that I was angry at her out of the blue. I was fat, but I think she was also going through some kind of insecurities about my growing up; you know, 'She's young, she's going to be beautiful, and here I am getting older.'"

"That happened later," said Ruth.

"I think it happened then, too, because there was a real nastiness going on between us. I would say, 'Oh, Mommy, do you think I'm fat and ugly?' She'd say, 'Well, if you'd lose ten pounds you wouldn't be.' And she'd say, 'Do you think I'm looking older?' And I'd say, 'Yes, but don't worry, it happens to everyone.' We were very good at subtly reinforcing each other's insecurities."

Ruth recalled, "A bit later, when Shelley stopped having a little-girl body and first had very noticeable breasts, I suddenly felt disturbed, threatened, and even resentful. I didn't think I would ever feel that way. It wasn't only competitive; the loss of a little girl bothered me. My charming child was gone, and all these problems were coming instead. Also she was growing up, so I was growing old, and all the competitive, envious, disturbed feelings rose up in me because she had breasts. But I don't remember our being that vicious with each other." To Shelley, she said, "I do remember saying to you that you should lose some weight, because you were very unhappy, and later you said, 'Mother, I couldn't sleep because you said I should lose weight.' I thought, 'I will never mention it again.' And I don't think I did."

Ruth was able to recognize and deal with her feelings. Problems arise when a mother's feelings of competitiveness become so strong that she is not able to let her daughter go. It may be that the habit of control is so strong that she cannot bear to give it up and recognize her daughter as a separate person who must make her own kind of life. Or she may overidentify with her daughter to the point of living vicariously through her experiences. Whatever the reasons, if she has not been able to develop a clear sense of her own identity in its various aspects—personal, sexual, social—her daughter's adolescence becomes a time when, instead of letting her go, she may find herself attempting to hold on to her by behavior that violates the boundaries of age, generation, and self. She may be doing this because she cannot give up her own past, because the present is unsatisfactory, or to stave off a future in which her role as mother will be phased out.

Boundary-violating takes many forms. It is most obvious on the level of direct sexual competitiveness, in which the jealousy and insecurity that Ruth Sampson expressed are not recognized, and so begin to interfere with a daughter's development. Boundary-violating is almost ensured by a society that expects mothers to give up any sense of their own lives "for the sake of" their children and husbands. The more a mother clings, the more her daughter will have to struggle to get free. Thus, by denying a mother any support for a life of her own, our society promotes boundary-violating and, so, promotes the more extreme forms of adolescent rebellion. A certain degree of turning away from a mother is bound to take place anyway, but when this turns into rebellion for its own sake, into behavior that often becomes self-destructive on a daughter's part, it is a sign that a mother is unable to give up her daughter.

Martha Henderson's memory of that period in her life is particularly relevant: "My mother had told me that sex was beautiful, and nothing to be ashamed of. At fifteen, I fell in love with a boy and we used to neck a lot. We never went to bed, but it was a very sensuous relationship. I wrote everything down in my diary, and my mother read it. She also used to listen to my phone calls whenever she could. She was furious; she confronted me with my diary and demanded to know why I wasn't ashamed of myself. I reminded her that she had told me sex was beautiful, but it didn't cut any ice. I had started dating later than most of the other girls. At thirteen and fourteen I was overweight, and boys just weren't interested in me. After the fight over the diary, I started being attracted to boys my mother really disapproved of—foreigners, guys with less education, sleazy types. That really antagonized her."

Virginia Freeman is being careful to respect Amy's privacy because "I always felt my mother might just take over part of my life if I wasn't careful. She was an attractive woman, and she used to become friends with all the boys I brought home, even the 'unsuitable' ones. I don't think she really realized what she was doing, or how strong her sexual attraction was. I wasn't completely aware of it myself, but I resented it tremendously. She never understood that. She came in one night with her hair all down her back. I was about seventeen and I was with a young soldier who was very feisty and full of himself. He ran his hands through her hair. I was mortified at the terrible behavior on both sides."

Although Ruth Sampson admits to having been jealous of Shelley's budding sexuality, she did not violate any sexual boundaries, and so, when Shelley got upset about a sexual encounter at camp, she was able to turn to her mother for comfort.

"When you called me from camp that time, I was so flattered I think I was probably the proudest mother in New York. I would never imagine doing anything like that with my mother," Ruth said.

Shelley replied, "I called you because I didn't know what else to do, I was so upset."

To me she said, "I was completely innocent; I wasn't thinking about sex. I was sort of wanting to be with boys. I had had lots of friends who were boys until I was about eleven, and then they began to go off with girl friends. At this camp, there was a guy I liked, and I didn't know what to do, so I just followed him around. Actually he represented everything I didn't like: he smoked cigarettes, and he was a big stud. He asked me to sleep out with him, and I knew what it meant but I said 'sure,' and I rolled up my sleeping bag and sneaked off to the archery field, leaving my childhood behind. Nothing much happened; we kissed, and felt each other up. I didn't know how far I was supposed to go; I felt very guilty about it, and finally I called my mother."

Ruth took up the story: "The phone rang, from Vermont, and it took Shelley about ten minutes to tell me she had been making out with a boy she liked. I said, 'Oh?' and she heard the alarm in my voice. She said, 'Oh mommy, don't worry, I'm too sensible for that.' So I asked her what she meant by making out, and she said kissing and hugging, and asked if that was okay. I said, 'Well, did you enjoy it?' She said she guessed so. I asked her if she thought she and the boy could still be friends and enjoy each other, and she said yes, so I said, 'Well then, what's wrong with it? You had a pleasant time.' She said, 'Oh thank you; I feel so much better.' And I felt so much better that she could talk about it."

Clothes have been, and remain, a classic arena for boundary-violating, since they are an important way for women to express their attractiveness. Several older women told me they remembered how their mothers would refuse to let them dress attractively, thus curbing the competition for the time being.

Ellen recalled, "My mother wanted me to dress in a way that was completely out of style, the way she would have dressed my sister, who was much older. She had a big thing about controlling clothes; she always had to choose them. She kept insisting I wear braids when nobody wore them anymore, and I had to wear those big sturdy oxfords when everyone else was wearing flats, and I couldn't wear pants when everyone else was. I used to say that she was ruining my life, and I always felt like a real ass. And she was very miserly about money; everybody else got cashmere sweaters for Christmas, and I never did. We used to have screaming fights about that, and my mother would say the other girls were just vain and stupid, that clothes were a big waste of money, and I should really be at boarding school and wearing a uniform."

One wonders to what extent this complaint hides or incorporates a deeper feeling that in her insensitivity to her daughter's needs, a mother is denying her daughter the emotional support that is so important at this period in her life.

Changing fashions and the youth cult of the 1960s have turned the tables. Now, teenagers' mothers are more likely to be dressing like them, violating the boundary between generations by letting their daughters set the pace and trying to follow. It is hard to blame mothers for this behavior when society provides few images of a strong, dignified middle age for women. But, understandably, daughters seem not to like it much.

Shelley talked about this problem. "Mothers are trying so much to look like their daughters that there is not so much for the daughters to rebel against. Mothers are all wearing blue jeans, as if they're rebelling against themselves. It's crazy; they walk around in peasant blouses looking younger than we do; they look ridiculous. They diet constantly; my mother has been on a diet ever since I've known her. I like it that they try to look their best; I think it's nice when they don't just let themselves go because they're married and don't have to look attractive to anyone else. I think it's good that my mother is taking a dance class; it keeps her in shape. But she doesn't go as far as blue jeans. When my friends' mothers come in with these outfits, my friends will say, 'What are you wearing? Get it off!' And the mothers will say, 'But it looks nice! All my friends are wearing it.' But we think they ought to look like mothers. I'm definitely in favor of the generation gap. It bothers me to go shopping and see old women in my department. I guess it's because I'm young, and I don't want them being young while I am. They've had their time. I don't feel they're competing, but just trying to get into something that they can't. They're very phony, somehow."

Overidentifying with a daughter can go much further than wearing the same clothes. Overinvestment in her achievements and living vicariously through her experiences are more subtle ways of trying to take over, of not being able to let go. Again, this can lead to the point where the daughter feels she doesn't have a life she can call her own.

Connie Maguire recalls running into this kind of problem when she was in her teens. "An awful thing happened as I got older; she began to get proud of me, but she would tell people about what I was doing in a way that made it seem *she* had done them. She had made it all possible, had encouraged me and given me the moral fiber to succeed. That was very hard for me. I think in a way she was reinforcing my sense of guilt—it was part of reminding me of all she had done for me. She believed firmly in the tradition of sticking to your husband no matter what and in giving up everything for your children. She constantly told me that she was doing everything for me and that her life was miserable as a result.

"At the same time, if I was a sterling human being, *she* had done it—it was her achievement. I felt like she was appropriating part of my identity. She would often describe my achievements in terms of her having done it first. She would talk about how bright she had been in high school. She came from a poor farm family, and she was very conscious of the fact that she was the smartest person in her high school. I can understand her feeling, but in a way she was telling me that my getting good marks wasn't such an achievement, because she had done it first. Even if it was something completely outside her own experience, such as my going to Europe as an exchange student, she would say, 'Oh, this is to be expected from *my* child.' In a way that was all right, but there was still a feeling of her not wanting just to participate in my achievements but to diminish them. Somehow she implied that they didn't really mean anything."

More extreme forms of boundary-violating can lead to a denial of a daughter's emotional autonomy, of her separate existence. R. D. Laing, in *The Politics of the Family*, shows how some mothers falsely describe their daughters to their faces: "*My* little girl would never feel that way."[5] Over a

period of time, daughters come to distrust their own feelings, believing instead what their parents say. This kind of
misrepresentation of one's feelings is emotionally analogous
to the physical boundary-violating, such as regimented or
forced feeding, that was discussed in Chapter III. In either
case, the child has no chance to discover her own identity;
she remains a sort of colony of her mother, who may be
colonizing her precisely because she has no strong sense of
her own separate self. Extremes of this situation can lead to
psychosis, drug addiction, or anorexia nervosa in adolescence. Anorexia is a condition that occurs mainly among
adolescent girls, and consists of a refusal to eat or retain
food.[6] Psychologists suggest that these symptoms represent
a refusal or inability to break the symbiotic tie with the
mother, a tie that should have begun to loosen at the age of
six months. Ironically, many girls who develop anorexia
have been "good girls," rarely in conflict with their mothers;
they simply seem never to have been able to develop a sense
of themselves as separate persons.

So many teenage daughters have had their diaries and
mail read, their choice of clothes and so forth controlled, that
these appear to be almost "normal" forms of boundary-violating. Too many mothers have not been able to arrive at that
kind of security of self that enables them to see, acknowledge, and support their daughters as separate people. Yet,
many mothers are trying to make the transition from over-
closeness, or "smother-love," to a recognition of themselves
and their daughters as separate individuals. This involves
growing pains for both mothers and daughters.

Grace Raphaelson is thirty-nine. Her daughter Helen, at
twelve, has just begun menstruating but is not yet interested
in boyfriends. The Raphaelsons live in a spacious suburban
house on Long Island. Grace has recently begun working
again as a department-store buyer. She told me, "I bought
the fantasies of marriage, housewife, apron, daddy coming
home. He would support us financially and I would be the
mother. It was a great disappointment to me to find that

motherhood wasn't fulfilling. My mother was always a working woman; she wasn't inclined to motherhood at all, and she made no bones about it. Work was more gratifying to her than having children; we were a nuisance. I kept thinking, 'I'm not going to do this to my children; I'm going to stay home, be there for them.' But it didn't work, because I was using the same bad techniques. Now I think just being home isn't the answer; one hour of being really together is worth a year of being together in disharmony. My mother manipulated all of us; she would overreact to everything and make us feel guilty by laying down ultimatums. She made me feel extremely bad about myself; she would call me names. Whatever I did wasn't good enough. If I got a C instead of failing, she would say it was terrible—'You never do anything as well as your older sister.' Now, when I get angry, I insult Helen and call her names. 'You stupid child, how could you do such a thing?' And she will call me names too, like, 'You jerk!' Then I threaten to take away something that I know I really can't take away, like, 'If you say one more thing you can't go to that party.' So of course she will say the one more thing.

"I haven't yet really learned that I am not Helen. I *am* her; she's like another arm, another foot. But now I'm trying to let go of her, to say, 'You are a person.' I was never a person to my mother; what I said didn't count. I was completely manipulated by her. I manipulate Helen, and Helen tries to manipulate me. She'll say, 'Even though you punish me now, you know you're going to let me go to the party anyway.'

"My husband had a temporary business transfer last year, and I decided that the children and I would stay here. That was one of my first really independent moves. For the first time in my life I began to think, 'I am not part of a package, I am an individual.' Which I don't think I was ever allowed to say. And I've been doing the same thing to my daughter. Up until now I wanted her to do what I wanted, just as my mother wanted me to do what she wanted. Then I became involved in my own work; I had to learn to stand on my own

two feet, and I'm beginning to see that Helen has to also. I
was always afraid to be aggressive because I saw my mother
as the dominating one in the family; my father was subservi-
ent to her. But now I realize that being an aggressive woman
doesn't have to mean castrating a man.

"If you have another foot or arm, you have control over it.
When Helen gets out of control, I feel, 'My God, that's my
foot, what is it doing? I can't let it do that.' But I'm beginning to see that I've got to separate myself from her, and
from my mother too.

"And I'm learning. The other day we were shopping;
Helen hates to try on clothes, and she's at a stage where she
is hard to fit. A saleswoman who had been very good at
fitting her before came over, and I said, 'Am I glad to see
you.' Helen said, 'Oh, not her again!' loud enough for the
saleswoman to hear. I am one of those people who would
never say anything derogatory for fear a stranger might
react negatively toward me. So here I was smiling and saying, 'Glad to see you,' and here was my other leg kicking this
woman in the shins. I was embarrassed, and then I said to
myself, 'Helen is not me. *I* am not insulting this woman, *she*
is.' However, as a parent, I really don't approve of that. As a
parent—but not as this other leg—I have to say something
to Helen. And I did."

VI

ENEMIES AND FRIENDS

In this chapter I am going to let three pairs of mothers and daughters speak for themselves about the problems adolescence has raised in their lives. I shall intervene only occasionally to make some observations. These three families certainly do not represent the whole range of situations that occur at this age; they were chosen to explore some of the ways in which changes in society and in the lives of mothers are affecting mothers and their late-adolescent daughters.

Marjorie Gordon represents the traditional mother, who has seen the recent changes in society reflected in the lives of her two younger daughters. Barbara Levine made abrupt changes in her own life that had serious repercussions on her daughter's life and on their relationship. Mary Robertson began early to combine her own independence with her role as a mother. Her daughter has drawn considerable strength from this.

Marjorie Gordon and her husband have raised five daughters. We have already met Marjorie and her oldest daughter, Sylvia, in Chapter V. Eighteen-year-old Julie, their youngest, is going through the pains of a late-adolescent rebellion. Mrs. Gordon has never worked; she has devoted herself to raising her daughters, but she doesn't feel that she has sacrificed herself for them. She believes in what are now considered the old-fashioned virtues: an ordered life, respect for others, family unity. She herself comes from a large family; her married daughters live nearby and visit frequently. Marjorie has a strong sense of the differences between her identity and responsibilities as a mother and her identity as a person in her own right. I spoke with her and with Sylvia and Julie, together and separately, and was struck by how close they remained while managing to respect each other's individuality.

"I was very conscious of wanting my daughters to be strong, independent people," Marjorie Gordon recalls. "I always thought that if I could give them self-confidence and enthusiasm, everything else would follow."

Sylvia vouches for her success. "It must have worked, because I was never afraid of anything, even though I don't remember thinking of myself as very competent. In seventh grade, I remember standing up for my girl friend when a boy was bullying her, and saying, 'If you come near her I'll beat you up!' "

Mrs. Gordon has raised all her daughters within the confines of traditional femininity. She recalls enjoying the traditional feminine activities—sewing, cooking, and shopping for clothes—with them. Her daughters were brought up to become wives and mothers, and the three oldest have done so. With the two youngest, however, things have changed. Both have been affected by the changing styles of adolescence that began with the youth culture in the 1960s and culminated in the vote for eighteen-year-olds.

"Our first three children were raised in a more or less conventional way that was bolstered by society," Marjorie said. "They were taught discipline and respect for authority in school as well as at home. I believe in the family virtues, and I like a gracious way of living; I tried to instill that in our daughters. As far as the outside world was concerned, our first three daughters were raised in an unruffled atmosphere; all mothers wanted their daughters home one hour after the dance. Of course, they did rebel in some ways; I don't think you can go through adolescence without some rebellion. And it's probably more bitter between mothers and daughters because we are both female. Up until then, a mother has been in the position of telling her daughter what she can and can't do, and a daughter no longer accepts that; she wants her own way. But we didn't really have problems until my fourth daughter came along. She began pioneering. The first three had always worn dresses to school; she insisted on wearing pants. At fifteen or sixteen discipline began to go. She was sneaking out after she was supposed to be in bed—something the first three never would have thought of doing. She wanted to 'do her thing,' and we didn't approve. But we had to face the fact that we were dealing with a different age in society. We couldn't keep her from wearing pants when everyone else was. We had to change our values."

"The world has really changed," Sylvia commented. "With the first three of us, it was all kind of peaceful. I was headstrong, and we had problems, but things were easier then. We weren't given as much freedom as kids are today; I was rebelling for little things, like later hours. Then along came the other two kids, and they were doing everything. We had to get married before we were allowed the freedom they have."

"This is a natural age to rebel, and getting the vote makes it worse," said Mrs. Gordon. Now they can drink at eighteen, and that's opened up a whole new social scene. Julie says that we should have no concern about where she goes or what she does. She tells us, 'I'm legal, I'm independent.' But of course she's not. And she isn't living up to her responsibilities to contribute to the household chores either.

"Our fourth child, Betty, left home at eighteen and has never been back to live. She dropped out of school and moved to Boston; she wanted to get her own apartment and go to school there, but we told her we couldn't afford to support her in her own apartment. We were prepared to pay for tuition for college here, and we wanted her in college. But she decided to stay there and get a job. Now she is thinking about college again and will do it on her own. When she left she was pioneering, fighting for the same personal freedom my youngest daughter has always had. Yet Betty always maintained some respect for us and for our ideas; although she didn't agree with them she wouldn't out-and-out defy them, as Julie does. She took the idea of independence very seriously. When she wanted to leave, she did. Julie is always threatening to leave, but she never really does. She goes off and stays with a girlfriend for a few days, and then comes back. Her disrespect, and her behavior, make me angry. I really think an eighteen-year-old should be out of the house; then, however she uses her freedom, she'll learn. I knew Betty would be all right; she is a very sound person, and sensible."

Later, Julie presented her own point of view: "When you get to be a teenager, you try to become your own person; you try to lose the mother–daughter situation and make a woman-to-woman situation instead, and that turns out to be touchy on both sides. I do things my way, and she does things hers, and we're both going to insist on our own way."

"The only thing you have to remember is that it's your parents' house," remarked Sylvia. "You're going to have to save your way for later."

"Yes," said Julie, "but then I feel stifled, like I have to get away."

"Well, that's just something you have to put up with," replied the pragmatic Sylvia.

Julie will be leaving for college in the fall, and it is probable that in the end she and her mother will become friends. At the moment, however, she is still ambivalent. She wants her own way, but she isn't ready to take on the responsibility for her own life. Mrs. Gordon feels ready to let her go, but Julie can't yet let go of her. She has a lot of freedom compared to her older sisters, but no way of using it constructively. Her mother has maintained her role as mother, without being hidebound about it. She says, "In the last few years I have become a lot more mellow, recognizing that there is nothing I can do about changing times. I think a lot of what is happening with women is very good, but some things are happening too fast. Teenage sex is perhaps too early."

She is worried about the effects of undisciplined freedom on her youngest daughters' generation: "What will this generation be like at thirty-five, having taken off and traveled or whatever instead of going to college or getting a job? Or if they go overboard with drugs, what effect will it have on the future? Or will sexual permissiveness destroy a relationship or a marriage?"

However, she has accepted the fact that Betty lives with a man to whom she is not married, although she admits to feeling ambivalent about it. When Julie has gone, she plans to get a job: "I have ten or twenty years left to work. But I do wish that I had had some experience, so I would have more confidence to go out now. If I were young now, I'm not saying I would be a flag-waver or a pioneer, but I certainly would embrace many of the feminist ideas."

Why, then, is Julie's rebellion so intense and personal? She seems to be engaging in boundary-violating, wanting her mother to change, to let her run the household her own way. If Mrs. Gordon were to do that, she would be abdicating her own position as mother and mistress of the household. As long as Julie is at home, Marjorie feels she must remain her mother.

Conflict generated by a clash between a permissive society and a traditional family is not confined to daughters, of course. But the expression of rebellion in domestic terms— who runs the household—is. Boys may protest rules about social life and so forth, but domestic activity can become a focus of conflict between mothers and daughters in a way that is unique to that relationship. Part of the problem may be that the meeting-ground between mother and daughter is confined to the home. Greater freedom demands a wider scope for responsible activity if it is not to degenerate into the kind of aimlessness that Mrs. Gordon fears. So far Julie has escaped having to face this necessary connection. She is in a kind of limbo—she has something to reject, but no clear idea of what to put in its place. Perhaps that is part of the reason why she stays at home and in conflict with her mother; that, at least, is concrete. Her rebellion is a way of maintaining a connection she is afraid to give up, while at the same time denying it. Her older sister Betty, perhaps because her freedom was more hard-won, was able to make a clean break—she separated from her mother and from her mother's way of life all at once.

Mrs. Gordon cannot be faulted for maintaining her own sense of herself and the values in which she believes. As she points out, her way of raising her older daughters was supported by society. Whatever the cost to them in terms of a muting of personal assertiveness, at least there was continuity between their mother's expectations and society's, and both pointed toward the same future. Mrs. Gordon's firm sense of herself and of her role will probably stand Julie in good stead when she does leave home and begins to lead her own life, whatever that may be.

Most adolescent daughters, as we have seen, want their mothers to keep to certain boundaries. The boundaries between the generations are important; the boundaries of the self are crucial. Yet, as with Julie Gordon, rebellion for daughters may mean resorting to a kind of boundary-violating of their own, whereby they want to turn the generation gap upside down, or make their mothers into someone they are not, or simply compete for their roles or domestic territory.

When a mother's traditional role is no longer supported by society, a discontinuity is created that can be resolved either by the mother's sticking to her traditional ideas as Mrs. Gordon did—or by her changing her role to create a new kind of relationship with her daughter, a more flexible one in which some traditional ideas of generational boundaries may appear to be violated but in which the changing realities of two distinct people are kept clearly defined. A greater degree of personal communication may exist in such relationships than in the more traditional mother–daughter relationship, in which, by the time the daughter reaches adolescence, she and her mother are leading parallel, but not frequently interconnecting, lives.

A real problem comes, however, when a mother drops the boundaries altogether, abdicating her role as mother before a daughter is ready for it. There is a natural time for such abdication, as Mrs. Gordon wisely observed. But as women reach out for more meaningful lives a conflict can arise between their own needs as developing people and their children's needs. Younger mothers, with small children, are attempting to work these problems out quite deliberately, as we have seen, and to the extent that they are consistent they may well be successful. But when a mother decides to change her way of living later in life, when her daughter is older and accustomed to a certain kind of mothering, conflicts will develop.

Barbara Levine is forty-five. Six years ago, she gave up a conventional suburban marriage to move to the city with her two young daughters. She went into business for herself, and although she'd never had a job before, she was successful. As she described it, she got married and had children without thinking too much about it, in the way that women always have been encouraged to do. As a suburban mother, she quickly discovered the "suburban pleasures of golf, bridge, and a full-time maid. So I was really almost neglecting my children. In retrospect, it seems to me that my desire to have babies was a feeling that I myself wasn't enough; I wanted to fill myself up. But they obviously didn't fulfill me, although I loved and wanted them.

"When we moved to the city, I was supporting the household; I felt like I had the weight of the world on my shoulders. It was good for me. It made me take myself seriously, but the children were neglected. I couldn't handle their needs; I was closed off to them.

"Rachel at fourteen or fifteen had to cook dinner, do the marketing, and take care of her sister. She was really the mother, and then when I came home and wanted to be the mother she resented it. The last two years were absolute hell. I was trying to be more concerned as a mother and was trying desperately to be a mother to her and to make up for what I hadn't been able to do before. She was having none of it. She would slam doors, argue—once she even threw me on the floor."

Rachel recalls, "When we first moved to the city my sister and I were very much on our own; Mother had a new boyfriend, and her work. I took a lot of responsibility for my sister. I had a lot of anger in me, I guess because I felt rejected. Then when she wanted to turn around and be a mother, I didn't understand it. Part of me really wanted a mother. I was confused. I let it out by yelling about the dishes."

There was also sexual competition between mother and daughter: Barbara had a lover whom both daughters resented, because his relationship to her was more that of another child and therefore a rival than of a father-figure for the girls. Rachel recalls that "she had to divide her love up; he couldn't relate to her as our mother, and we couldn't relate to her as his lover." At fifteen, partly in retaliation, Rachel began sleeping with her own boyfriend, who was several years older than she. For a while he moved in with the family. Barbara recalls, "I didn't mind her sleeping with him, but he wasn't working, and he made no contribution to the household."

Rachel says that "she couldn't relate to the fact that I was having a really serious relationship with a man; it wasn't just having a boyfriend. She told me once she felt it was all just starting for me, which meant it was all ending for her. That bothered her. I think partly the reason I got so involved with my boyfriend was to make my mother uptight; it was like slapping her in the face. I used to do a lot of things just to make her uptight."

At seventeen, Rachel moved into her boyfriend's apartment. "One night we were arguing," said Barbara, "and I said, 'Oh, don't give me such a hard time!' and she walked out the door. She was gone. She was barely seventeen; I was nervous and frightened about it, but on the other hand it was very peaceful and quiet with just my other daughter and me here. And it has worked out; it's a miracle. She and I immediately liked each other better because we didn't see each other every night. She is supporting herself, and she's going to college next year. Recently she came for dinner and said, 'How come everything is so pleasant when a few weeks ago you hated me?' I told her I never hated her; that she had been giving me a hard time at every turn, and was generally being horrible. Some of the time I deserved it, but much of the time it was her problem."

Rachel's view is that "I was miserable when we were living together; because we don't really live the same way. Now that I'm on my own, I live my own way. If the dishes build up, it doesn't bother me; she would get angry and start yelling at me. I'm more my own person now. I like responsibility; I like taking care of myself. And lately we've been getting along well; she's proud of me again. Before, I was the problem and my sister was the good daughter.

"Part of the problem was my independence. I had a lot of freedom. At fourteen I traveled around the country by myself. But I needed that freedom; without it I think I might have run away and never come back. It was groovy because when I needed her I would call her, and I always let her know where I was."

Barbara says, "Looking back now, I can see that I was really afraid of her; I simply couldn't cope. I was too permissive; now I think permissiveness is the easy way out. For me, it was a way of assuaging the guilt I felt over having neglected her. With my younger daughter, I'm not afraid to put my foot down." It took Barbara a long time to reassert boundaries; the conflict with Rachel was a time of growth for her, also, and she has found herself able to provide her younger daughter with firmer support and authority.

Rachel still feels ambivalent about the situation. On the one hand, she feels she needed a lot of freedom; on the other hand, she would have liked her mother to be more consistently firm from the beginning. "Moving out only helps if the daughter is in the frame of mind to change herself. If you can leave and still be friends with your parents, then it's good. I have friends who will never see their parents again, mostly because their mothers were too protective. When the daughters left, they left for good.

"I think the line between mother and friend is basically the issue between mothers and daughters. My mother can't always define the line between being my friend and being my mother. The mistake she made was to put her foot down after letting everything slide. If she had been more consistent I wouldn't have had as much hostility. Maybe if I'd had less freedom I would have gotten more out of school and being a teenager." It is a tribute to both mother and daughter that their communication has remained good; moving out is not possible for all daughters who feel intense conflict with their mothers, but clearly Rachel was mature enough to handle this rather drastic step.

Both Rachel and Julie have found themselves involved in intense conflict with their mothers, and both daughters have themselves become boundary-violators. But Rachel's mother in a sense invited boundary-violating by abdicating her role as mother; Julie's mother, on the other hand, has tried to maintain her authority in the face of rapidly changing social mores. Rachel moved out, and Julie is obviously ready to leave home; both their mothers are wise enough to perceive the need for letting their daughters go when the time comes.

The letting-go process between Mary Robertson and her daughter Jane has been more gradual. By some standards, they represent a radical life style. Mrs. Robertson is divorced and for many years has had a successful career as a documentary-film maker. Jane, now seventeen, has been working with her mother and receiving film credits since she was fourteen. They are extraordinarily open with each other, able to discuss their differences within a context of great respect for each other as separate individuals.

In the best sense of the word, then, the Robertsons are quite conservative: they live an ordered and comfortable life, and they work hard and respect each other. Mary has never been permissive; that is, she has never abdicated her responsibility as Jane's mother. What she has done is to create a situation in which she and Jane can relate to each other as mutually developing people in an evolving relationship founded on mutual support and affection. As a result, Jane has never found real rebellion necessary.

Because Mrs. Robertson early on decided that she was going to be her own person without giving up her responsibilities as a mother, she has related to Jane on those terms, seeing her as both her daughter and a person in her own right, able to take an increasing amount of responsibility for herself but still subject to a gradually diminishing degree of parental control. There has never been the sudden sharp break between an old pattern and a new one that the Levines suffered. Although many of the personal values of the Robertsons seem strikingly similar to those of the Gordons, domestic life has been only one aspect of the relationship between mother and daughter. They are very close, but there is less of the confrontation between generations that characterizes Julie and Marjorie Gordon's relationship. Jane Robertson has grown up with an evolving sense of responsibility both at home and in her mother's work.

"What has affected my relationship with Jane, I think, is my deciding that I was going to live the way I wanted to live," said Mary. "That has meant I was able to decide that Jane didn't need to be exactly like me; if I want to be an individual, then I have to allow my daughter to be one. It's not so much an intellectual decision as an emotional one.

When she was very tiny I was still on that repetitive track; if I was like my mother then Jane would be like me. Then at some point everything began opening up. Part of it was deciding to get divorced; that opened some doors in my life, and then it was just basically doing what I thought was right.

"I think doing your own thing as a mother makes it a lot easier on a daughter. Then the daughter isn't a project. She isn't your connection with the world, or your source of power, or your reason for living. Luckily there was a point, very early, when I was able to give up my daughter. Now there is such a lovely, flowing momentum, as I grow and as she grows up. My life is not a constant—I'm changing too."

"I think it's really important to see your mother change," said Jane. "I think most of my friends have been rebelling against mothers who haven't changed. They see their mothers as being the same thing forever; so it's either rebel or be just like them, instead of both of you evolving and continuously relating."

"I think the ideal thing is to share in the situation," Mary added. "But there are some areas where a mother has to be in charge, and say, 'Trust me.' But you don't do that any more than you have to. It has to be a very drastic situation."

"The last time was at camp, don't you think?" said Jane. "I went to a camp where all the swimming was in the nude. I was just sixteen, the youngest person there. When Mommy came up and found out about it she decided it was not a good thing, that she didn't approve of it, and she took me out of the camp. I wanted to stay. And I still think, Mommy, that no matter what you thought of it, it was important for me to finish the summer. I had gotten so many relationships going, and I was really a leader. But I didn't have any choice."

"Why did you think this was a bad thing?" I asked Mary.

"It was very hard. I didn't do it right away, but when I got home I thought, this might be upsetting her without her realizing it. You can't tell kids of sixteen that they are not aware of what they are really feeling. I thought it was a very unhealthy situation; the counselors seemed awfully hung up. It's like predicting that your daughter will get raped if you leave her in a certain situation. Whether she understood it or not, I knew I had to act. It's a very good thing that we had a connecting relationship before that; you can't do something that will really cut off communication between you. But I had to act according to my conscience and my sense of what happens to feelings; I thought if I didn't do something I would be a very weak person. Her approval of me was not important; the important thing was her psyche. I knew we could straighten it out with each other eventually, and I think we have; don't you, Jane?"

"It's hard," replied Jane. "I was furious. You could have let me know that you felt that way without taking me out of the camp."

"I don't think I could have. It seemed like it required some action, because no matter what I felt, it wasn't going to change what was happening to you. Boy, I learned a lot."

It is interesting to compare Jane's present position with Julie Gordon's and Rachel Levine's. The example of Mary's life has provided Jane with a number of interesting options for her future. Julie has not had such examples provided for her, and so must seek them out on her own. Rachel seems caught between these two positions. Her rebellion was structured in the same intensely personal way as Julie's; both seemed bent on disrupting their mothers' lives. Yet, like Julie's sister Betty, Rachel was able to move out and take her search for options out of the arena of personal rebellion against her mother.

In Chapter II I cited Nancy Chodorow's theory that a healthy separation between mothers and daughters is most likely when daughters grow up in an environment in which mothers have a concrete, productive role in the world outside the home, yet where there is not such a rigid separation between home and work that it is impossible for mothers or

daughters to reconcile. Mary and Jane Robertson's relationship seems to bear out this theory. Of course, as I have
pointed out, the simple fact of a mother's working doesn't
necessarily make a difference—if she resents working, or
feels guilty about it, her feelings will be reflected in her
relationship with her daughter. The best possible situation
may be one in which home and work are brought as close
together as possible, admittedly a difficult project in today's
world, but one that Mary Robertson seems to have successfully accomplished.

"What do you want from your mother?" I asked Jane.

"Support, I think," she answered.

"Jane supports me, too," said Mary. "If something good is
happening, then eventually you grow to support each other."

"I remember last year, when Mommy had a new boyfriend
who moved in with all his things. I thought, 'Mommy's getting taken in. She's not aware of what she's getting herself
into; she should be a little more cynical.' Usually mothers
have to deal with their daughters' boyfriends; this was the
other way around. And I think more and more daughters
have those feelings. I want to protect her in the same way
she wants to protect me."

"That's a nice thing," said Mary, "because you trade a
sense of your feelings, and of being concerned—a sense that
you know what's happening, even though you wish that the
person would do something differently."

"I feel I also support her in her work," added Jane. "It's
her job, but it's the family's business; it's ours, too. I've been
involved in a lot of the productions, answered phones, dealt
with temperamental directors, and so on. Most of my friends
flip out at this, because they're breaking their ties with their
mothers in different ways, and I still have all these very
secure ties. Working with and for your mother, supporting
your mother, is a hard thing. Some of my friends' mothers
don't work, and have devoted a lot—maybe too much—of
their time to their children. Then you can't work with your
mother, because you have to break away from her. I think

Mommy broke away from me before I broke away from her. I've had feelings of resentment at getting less attention, but she wouldn't have been able to give me what she has if she hadn't broken away."

"I decided that whatever work I did had to be a family project," said Mary, "because otherwise I didn't know how we could really swing it. And then I found out that my daughter at fourteen was so much more a person, and so much more grown up or grown into doing things than most people I could hire. That's fun, and much better."

It isn't always easy to have a mother who is a strong person in her own right, however, particularly when you also work with her. Jane and I talked about how she handles some of her problems in breaking away from her mother. Her primary concern is to get other people to deal with her as herself, rather than as her mother's daughter.

"When I'm feeling insecure, and having doubts about someone, then it's hard to have my mother around, because she's so beautifully critical. I'm the same way with her friends. There is a while, in the beginning of friendships, when you want to have them be your friends, and not your mother's. Her boyfriends are more parents to me, or friends. But I don't want her to deal with my boyfriends as her sons. The first time I had sex I didn't tell her. It seemed like something I wanted to talk to my girlfriends about and not my mother. I was sixteen, and I had a boyfriend sleep over here. But I don't feel so comfortable about having sex in my mother's house, especially when she's here.

"Also, she's very strong, and it's easy for her to scare someone. People of sixteen and seventeen aren't that sure of who they are; sometimes they aren't comfortable enough with themselves to be able to accept a woman who is very strong, and then I get uptight about it. She always says just what she thinks; I like that, but it's harder for other people to deal with.

"I want to be a very separate individual; lots of times people deal with me as her daughter instead of as myself, and I don't like that. Obviously, if someone knows Mommy through business, then I'm her daughter. I just try to impress upon them the fact that I'm another person, and how they can deal with me in other ways. At the same time, I think there are times when you like to be your mother's daughter. When you're in a situation where you're not in control—away from the protection of home and school—it's easier to have somebody's hand to hold, to have an identity when you're not sure of who you are."

Jane has a very clear image of the kind of woman she would like to become; it is, she says, very much like her mother. "I think 'feminine' can be anything. You can be very feminine and at the same time be forceful and strong; strength can be gentleness. It's also very masculine to be very strong and yet very gentle. It's really a question of *why* you are doing things, rather than what you are doing. It can be very feminine to build your own house, depending on what it's expressing. Being a woman is rooted in your sexuality; if you feel very much a woman and you can express it, then anything you do is expressing your femininity; it's just there."

VII

MEN, MARRIAGE, MOTHERS

Women are changing their lives, and as their lives change so does the way they relate to men—and to their daughters. It should be clear by now that what a woman thinks of herself will have a profound effect on her relationship with her daughter and on her daughter's subsequent relationships with men.[1]

Relationships with men may embody a battle for possession of oneself, which is really a continuation of a daughter's battle with her mother. The form of the conflict with men may be seen more in terms of sexual identity or gender-role difficulties, but in its bitterest forms it involves a battle for selfhood. When divorce was out of the question, women had no recourse but to suppress these conflicts by suppressing themselves. Increasingly, today, they are taking the option of separation and divorce, or of raising children on their own. Some women are able to change the structure of their marriages as they begin to develop a sense of themselves as persons. Some few have fled from heterosexuality altogether.

In this chapter, we shall look at some of these solutions and their effects on mother–daughter relationships.

If, early in life, a daughter does not receive enough support from her mother to develop a sense of herself, she may

never develop the self-assurance necessary for true heterosexuality, in which she must compete with her mother—and,
later, other women—for men. In competing with her mother,
she must also be able to feel sure that she won't lose her
mother's love; she must know that in separating from her she
can still, to some extent, keep her. This difficulty may be at
the root of many women's ambivalence about heterosexuality, and it may also explain in part why it is such a common
pattern for women to "lose themselves" in a relationship
with a man. As I mentioned in Chapter III, Freud pointed
out that the relationship with the father, and ultimately with
other men, is based upon the relationship with the mother.[2]
If, in that relationship, a daughter has not "found herself,"
has not been encouraged to develop a strong sense of personal and sexual identity, it will be much easier for her to
attribute selfhood to men and to behave in a relationship
with a man as though he were her mother, from whom she
has not separated. And because she has not separated from
her mother, she becomes dependent on the man, needing
from him all the reassurance of her own worth that she
needed from her mother, and perhaps never got. Or, she may
express toward men a hostility she really feels toward her
mother. In an extreme situation, she may find herself acting
mainly to please her mother. A man may serve as a sort of
buffer zone between a mother and daughter who aren't really separated at all.

Yvonne recalls that, although her mother worked, she dis-
liked doing so because she felt her husband should have
been able to support her. Consequently, she gave Yvonne
very ambiguous messages about what was expected of her.
On the one hand, she encouraged her to go to college, but on
the other hand, she was very concerned about her social life,
wanting her to put marriage and family first. Yvonne had a
conflict she couldn't resolve. She was influenced by her father, who was an intellectual, and by an older brother. But
underlying these identifications was the feeling that she had
never been sure of her mother's support for her as a separate

person. When Yvonne won a scholarship to a prestigious women's college she found the atmosphere of intellectually competitive women in the dormitory very frightening. So she left school. "I felt I had to get married; I wanted to please my mother more than anything in the world. I finally found a guy who met all my mother's qualifications; he was presentable, he had a good, professional-level job. But he didn't like women very much, and the sex wasn't too good. My parents had a very asexual relationship, I think; it was almost as if with my marriage I was reliving theirs. I was desperate to get married; I just wanted somebody in a business suit who looked presentable, whom I could take home to my mother and say, 'See, I did it; now leave me alone.'

"And it worked! I accomplished exactly what I wanted; he always came between my mother and me, and as long as I was with him she never crossed me. Then my husband and I separated, and I suddenly found that without him as a buffer zone I had become a target again. Recently my mother was visiting me, and my daughter was playing with paper on the floor. She picked up a pair of scissors to cut it, and my mother tried to prevent her. She began lecturing me about not letting Vicki use scissors, because they were too dangerous. I exploded. I suddenly realized that I am a grown woman, with a good job, supporting myself and my daughter, and just because there was no husband there to tell my mother to get lost she was treating me like some recalcitrant child."

Yvonne's marriage was for form's sake only. She used it as a means of separating from her mother, thereby both winning her mother's approval for her social success in attracting and marrying the "right kind" of man, and creating, through the intervention of her husband, a distance from her mother that she hadn't been able to achieve on her own. But it didn't work; there was still no real psychological separation. Yvonne's choice of a man who did not like women and her remark about the absence of sexuality in both her parents' and her own marriage suggest that she was unsure of both her sexual identity and her personal identity. Her mother has never been able to give up her investment in her. Yvonne says, "She has reverted to her old habits of threatening that my behavior would finish her off. When she had a heart attack, she blamed it on the fact that I had a lover, and she didn't approve of that."

Lynn Carson, who gave up heterosexuality altogether, represents an even more extreme response to a binding mother–daughter relationship. For her, heterosexuality and a feminine gender role became synonymous, and equally destructive to her sense of herself as a person.

"I never did feel very feminine," she told me. "My mother treated me as an asexual person; she identified with me as being like herself as a little girl and tried to keep me as a young alter ego. I had to learn the feminine role by watching and studying other people: lipstick, nail polish, the works. My mother was very involved with all those things too, and it was all an overlay for her as well.

"She certainly is not very sexual; she told me not too long ago that she feels sexually inadequate and inexperienced. It's easy for me to intimidate her with my own sexual experience, and she loved it after I got divorced, when I went through a period of having lots of lovers. She's Jewish; for her, children are a replacement for lovers. Women aren't mothers and lovers, they're just mothers.

"She has a business career; she is a typical prefeminist career woman, very male-defined. She's prejudiced against hiring women because she thinks they will just get married. She passed on to me her own sense of conflict about the qualities demanded in a job and qualities expected of a woman.

"When I came out, a whole lot of things fell into place; getting rid of men cleared things up tremendously. I began to see that the threat of lesbianism is used as role enforcement; I saw the lengths to which women would go to stay inside a role. You could only go so far before you defined yourself as a freak or a maniac. Getting outside the role boundaries helped me to begin to see my mother; and her compromises no longer made any sense to me. She really believes that women are naturally weaker and more maternal than men. When I came out, I became aware that 'woman' and 'feminine' have nothing to do with each other. 'Feminine' is drag.

"I don't know whether it's possible to split 'woman' and 'femininity' and remain heterosexual. It depends on the kind of men you find to relate to, I suppose. I found that sex with men was fine, but I couldn't get outside of the roles."

Lynn's feelings are poles apart from the feelings expressed by Jane Robertson in Chapter VI, that femininity is rooted in your sexuality, and that if you feel yourself to be a woman anything you do is feminine. Jane's mother has never made the division between gender roles and personal and sexual identity. Because she was able to assert her own sense of personal and sexual identity, she was able to take gender roles lightly, as roles rather than as some elusive way of looking and behaving on which her whole sense of self depended. For Lynn's mother, the conventions of femininity, of gender role, bore the whole weight of identity. Lynn was perceptive enough to see beyond this to her mother's very real personal and sexual insecurity, which she then equated with the feminine role as her mother presented it to her. Paradoxically, the more intensely Lynn played the role, the more she felt it was disguising her own sexual and personal insecurity.

Lynn's story may make an important point about the difficulty of achieving identity as a woman in our society. Coming from a mother–daughter relationship in which there was little support for heterosexuality and in which she perceived that her mother was strongly conflicted about the double message, Lynn rejected heterosexuality altogether. "I became aware that 'woman' and 'feminine' have nothing to do with each other. 'Feminine' is drag." Lynn's mother was deprived of a strong sense of herself as a female; she overidentified with a masculine role and stressed the superficial aspects of femininity to compensate for her personal and sexual insecurity. For Lynn, then, relating to men meant having less of herself as a woman. Jane Robertson's mother, Mary, relates to men on her own terms, rather than in terms of some ideal role. She has found that she doesn't have to "shoehorn herself into the heterosexual relationship," as Lynn expressed it. Lynn says, "I felt femininity involved thinking of myself in terms of being dependent on some man for my whole life." Mary Robertson has somehow achieved just the opposite. She thinks of her own life and interests first, so heterosexuality has not become confused with roles and she has been able to support Jane's development as a separate person.

Unfortunately, our society is so involved with the concept of gender roles that they have become equated with the idea of self, in the mistaken belief that socially recognizable and acceptable behavior somehow indicates a secure sense of self. But women are beginning to question this equation. In getting married, both Yvonne and Lynn were playing roles, going through the motions, but their stories indicate how seriously our formalization of gender roles has gone awry. Both women's central involvement continued to be with their mothers. Their difficulties with men are, as I suggested in Chapter III, disguising their difficulties in separating from their mothers.

Our culture has encouraged women to define themselves in terms of their relationships with men rather than in terms of themselves and their relationships with each other. Conventional marriage works against a woman's expression of a strong sense of personal and sexual identity because it demands that she identify more strongly with her husband's interests than her own. The other side of the coin is the woman who wishes to achieve and finds herself identifying with a masculine role—perhaps, as with Lynn's mother, to the extent of a feminine identification that is negative. In either case, the feminine role has had no real room for a strong sense of personal and sexual identity that can be passed on to, and supported in, a daughter. But this is changing, slowly. The strongest sense of selfhood and of mutual respect that I observed in the mother–daughter relationships I explored appeared most often in situations in which mothers either had established themselves outside of a marriage, generally by getting divorced and deciding not to remarry, or had managed to structure a marriage that freed them from traditional role expectations. These mothers identified more strongly with their own interests than with their husbands', although they remained sympathetic toward and interested in their husbands' or lovers' activities. They had managed to resolve the conflict of the double message by seeing themselves as achieving women who can also relate to men.

Increasingly, women who have been raised with the kind of contradictions expressed by Lynn and Yvonne are choosing a third option: if they got married as part of fulfilling the usual expectations of femininity, they are getting divorced not in order to marry some other man but in order to sort out their own sense of themselves. It may be very difficult for mothers with an investment in the image, if not the reality, of a conventional marriage to accept a daughter's decision to divorce on these terms because when a daughter does divorce in the hope of discovering her own identity as a woman, she is separating from the image of femininity she received from her mother and from society, and in so doing she is questioning the very foundations of whatever compromises of identity her mother has made. In a way, she is not just divorcing a man; she is divorcing her mother as well.

Marcia Fried is thirty-five. In her first marriage she had two daughters. "My own mother was divorced when I was four and never remarried. She often held two jobs to support us both, so I never saw enough of her as a child; I spent a lot of time at neighbors' houses. I got married at seventeen and immediately had two children. I was into super-motherhood, always baking bread, and so forth, and my daughters tell me what a happy childhood they had; that makes me feel good. Then, when I was twenty-five, we separated, and I found myself with two children, no education, and no money. At that point I decided the time had come to do something for myself. My husband had been going to graduate school, and I hadn't even been to college. The girls were in school, so I got a job and began going to college part-time, at night. I discovered that I liked coping, after the first difficult period was over. It made me feel very resourceful.

"My mother wasn't at all supportive during my divorce; she made me feel very guilty. She couldn't handle it. She was projecting her guilt about me onto my behavior, instead of being able to identify with me and sympathize with what I was going through. After my divorce she didn't come to see me for about two years. Finally I told her she would just have to accept me as I was, rather than insisting on some ideal that was really something she hadn't been able to live up to, and felt guilty about."

Alex Brenner has two small daughters. She recalls, "My mother had a terrible marriage; she and my father fought all the time. And she made no demands on life; she chose to stay home, although I think she could have done something if she had wanted to. But instead she was always either angry, resigned, or feeling sorry for herself and crying. She has two daughters, and we are both divorced. She considers that it's her fault. She also thinks it's easier to stay married. The minute I told her my husband and I were separating she said, 'Nothing in marriage could be worse than being alone; look at all the troubles you're bringing on yourself. At least if you stay married, he'll support you. Do whatever you want, but let him support you, provide you with a home, and take care of you.'

"But she didn't really believe I could do whatever I wanted and stay married, because she would tell me, 'You've got to learn to compromise. It's not easy being married. Give in, it's better than not being married. You can't buck the system.'

"Now she is beginning to express great rage at me because I'm independent, I'm supporting myself, I'm beginning to do things she would have loved to do. So she's constantly making the kind of snide, put-down remarks that come from rage; she can't express her anger directly.

"I have had very little preparation to be alone and be part of the world, but now I'm the only one who stands between my daughters and disaster, so I have to be adequate. The whole point of my life now is learning to cope alone, so I don't see any reason to marry again. Except that I do worry about my daughters not seeing me in a good relationship with a man."

What happens to the relationship between a divorced mother and her daughter? Marcia's daughters are sixteen and seventeen; Alex's are four and five. Both found that one daughter was more attached to her father, and this has raised problems. Alex told me, "My younger daughter, Lizzie, has been going to pieces lately because my husband isn't here. She was much more attached to him than my older daughter was; in fact, by the end I felt we were divided into two families, Lizzie and my husband and Wendy and myself. Lizzie would run to her father, and say, 'I don't want you Mommy, I want my daddy!' But on the whole it is much more peaceful since John and I separated, because we aren't fighting. Wendy has told me she's glad that has stopped; that life is easier now. Lizzie still doesn't think it's worth it, but I'm beginning to get closer to her."

Marcia remembers that the hardest thing about her divorce was identifying with her daughters in their grief. "I went into therapy. I was reliving through my daughters my own childhood sense of loss; I was becoming *them.* They also had a lot of anger; they used to say that if I had been nicer Daddy wouldn't have left. I had to learn that I wasn't them, that they had more support from me than I had had from my mother, and that their father was still available to them."

Marcia eventually remarried. "I wanted to get married again; I still believed that was important. Now I'm not so sure. Possibly if feminism had come along earlier, I wouldn't have gotten married again right away. I need to have a close relationship with a man, but marriage isn't the only answer today."

Marcia's older daughter, Stephanie, found she had a difficult time accepting Bob, her stepfather. "She is most like me in temperament and looks," said Marcia, "and perhaps as a result she was closer to her father than Lisa was. I guess she really resented Bob, and they used to fight a lot. She was also very critical of me. I felt I was in a very bad position, because I couldn't completely side with either one. I would try to talk to them separately, and support both of them to create a compromise, but it never really worked. Finally, I spoke to her father and suggested she live with him, and now she does. I felt a real sense of failure when she left, although I knew it was the best thing for all of us. Now, though, she gets along better with Bob when she does see him, and her father isn't such an ideal, since she lives with him. She and I get along better, too."

Marcia was in the middle, caught between her husband and her daughter, and their conflict might eventually have boiled over into a direct conflict between mother and daughter. For Stephanie to move out put a strain on Marcia's sense of herself as a good mother, but she was realistic enough to see that living with her father would help Stephanie develop a perspective that was impossible for her to find otherwise.

Andrea Blaustein also has found herself in the midst of a conflict that is really between her husband and daughters, but she has decided to compromise in order to keep the peace. She is married to an insurance executive, and her daughters are fifteen and seventeen. She described how her husband's role expectations have affected her relationship with her daughters: "Husbands have certain expectations of their daughters and wives, so in order to get along with her husband, or please him, a mother will treat her daughter differently from the way she would if they were by themselves, and she were making the rules. Men feel they have to make the rules; my husband's values have primacy in the house.

"My husband is very fussy about things like table manners and a clean house; I'm not. He's always yelling at them to clean up their rooms, or keep their elbows off the table, and he expects me to back him up. I try to make compromises, but neither side will accept that. My inclination is to side with the girls; I sympathize with them, and identify with them more. But if I completely sided with them I would end up in a sort of conspiracy with them against him, and I don't like that either.

"So it's a conflict with them I wouldn't have if it weren't for him. And my daughters get mad at him because he wants me to tell them instead of telling them himself. He feels that if I don't back him up they'll disobey him because they'll know I don't agree with him.

"In a way, he's trying to insure that they'll be the right kind of women, who can be controlled by their husbands. The only way I'm really fighting it is with inertia. I always took it for granted that he shouldn't do anything in the house, and then when the women's movement came along I realized that things could be different, and that made it harder. The girls started saying, 'Why should we do it when Daddy doesn't do anything?' I tried to get him to do more things, but he insists that his role is to work, and do the fixing up.

"It gets pretty serious. I feel I have compromised myself, but I've been doing it for so long that I wasn't aware until recently of what had happened. I didn't feel ambivalent when the girls were little.

"Probably what really irritates him is that the girls are growing up and becoming individuals, and are more and more independent of him. He was raised mainly by women, and he probably resented them and felt they were smothering him, so maybe he wants his daughters to be subordinate to him, and they resist.

"Also, I think that in a way he has always been jealous of my relationship with my daughters; he wants his relationship with me to be primary."

Andrea has decided to stick it out on her husband's terms. She has her own work as a professional potter, and she doesn't think moving out at this point would really help herself or her daughters. Marcia was luckier. For her the solution to role problems has been to restructure the household: "In the past five years I have changed from being mainly concerned about home and family to being interested in graduate study and my own work." The family is run more like a sort of commune than a traditional family. In addition to Lisa, there are Bob's two sons. They all take turns with the domestic chores. Lisa and her mother have become closer in the last few years; Lisa thinks the reason has quite a lot to do with feminism: "My friends and I have all started talking to our mothers a lot more, and thinking about how they relate to feminism. When you start getting into feminism, and learning about women, you start asking, 'How does this relate to my mother?' I'm a young person, I've got my whole life. All the options are open. I began asking, 'Did my mother have the same options? How did she turn out the way she is? Will I turn out the same way?'

"Twenty years ago there wasn't much my mother could do but get married. I understand that, but I said she didn't need to remarry. She said she did, because she was lonely, and thought she needed the support of a marriage. I suppose I can see that. She hadn't done anything but be married, she wasn't trained for work.

"She's been changing a lot in the last few years; she's gotten involved in feminism herself, and we have that to talk about, although I'm a lot more radical than she is. But I'm getting more tolerant. I'm seeing that it's very hard to change your life style completely when you're thirty-five. I have to accept that. And she has made a lot of very positive changes, like going back to school, trying to do something with her life. That's hard, I don't know whether I could, if I had been in a house my whole life.

"I think I could live without having emotional relationships with men; I could find all my emotional needs satisfied by women. I think the needs are the same whoever you're relating to, but women aren't supposed to be friends. Women are competitors.

"My mother and I give each other moral support, because we're there, and we're sympathetic. We have conflicts about things like how clean the house should be, and about radical feminism. But basically we support each other. I can see that she's changing, and she's thinking; so now I can relate to her as a person.

"Basically, we agree on how a household should be run—that men should take part in it. Everyone here cooks, and we all help clean. Bob would prefer to live in a traditional household. He says, 'That's the way it's supposed to be,' and my mother says, 'That's not the way it is.' It's a real conflict for them."

Marcia told me, "Lisa has been very supportive in the past few years; I don't think I could have gotten along without that support. She has been a real friend; she empathizes a lot with my life. But I think she has a hard time understanding my relationship with Bob; he has been very tolerant and supportive of me and of the changes I've made in the family's life. He's not used to anything like this.

"My mother really didn't relate well to women; she was always a coquette. At the same time, she doesn't relate well to men, either, because of that coquette role. I like men, but I think my deepest trust is in women; I don't know what I would do without my women friends. I think Lisa has gotten some of her attitudes from me. My mother's attitude, on the other hand, was typical of a whole generation; they just didn't examine their lives as much."

Like Mary Robertson, Marcia Fried has created a situation in which her own needs as a person are not subordinated to her role as wife and mother. Unlike Mary, she has managed to do this within the context of marriage, by radically revising the way her household is run. But, like the Robertsons, Marcia and Lisa can strongly support each other because they see themselves and each other as persons.

Both mothers have stepped outside of the conventional feminine role boundaries, without needing to make the equation between "feminine" and "heterosexual" that caused Lynn to give up on men altogether. The line of support from mother to daughter is very strong and direct, and the question of relating to men is only one part of it.

It is probably much easier for a woman to make changes with a lover or a second husband than with a husband who has grown accustomed to traditional roles, as Andrea's has. Yet Ann Martinson has managed to restructure a first marriage to accommodate a career and, as we saw in Chapter IV, she and her daughter already have the kind of strong, supportive relationship that Lisa and Marcia have more recently developed. Partly this is because Ann's husband is more flexible and understanding than Andrea's, and seems less dependent on roles for his sense of identity. Ann's story also shows how a more traditional kind of mother–daughter closeness evolved between herself and her mother, Alicia Blair. The kind of split between women as supportive friends and men as husbands or lovers that Marcia Fried and her daughter expressed is not new; it has merely taken on different forms as women change their ways of relating to each other and to men.

Alicia Blair recalls, "I wanted to go to Cornell, but we couldn't afford it. Mother wasn't too much in favor of it; she was worn out. She wanted me to go to Wilson Normal School in Washington; the last thing I wanted to do was teach. So I enlisted in the navy. It was World War I, the first time the navy had taken women. Mother was shocked. Then, a year later, I was to go to Hawaii. I was dying to go, but Mother pitched such a fit that I didn't; I got out of it. She couldn't bear the thought of my living that far away from her. She wasn't well at the time, she was working, and she had my younger sister. I couldn't do it. But I resented it. I resented not going to college, and later there were many times when I could have, but I was too lazy. If I had gotten my degree I never would have married my husband; it was a perfectly wild adventure. He was mercury; everybody gave us six months, but we lasted twenty-five years.

"I was delighted to have Ann, because I didn't want a son. I have this resentment against men; you can't get around it. I think I saw too many dominating men when I was little—my grandfather and my uncles."

Alicia was widowed and living with her daughter when Ann got married. "I left after she got married. We were so close, she could look at me and know what I thought. You need some privacy to form a basis for a marriage. I never dreamed I would come back and stay with them."

"How do you think you and Ann developed this unspoken communication?" I asked.

"I think it was largely because we were always getting around her father. We were in league against him. There was a lot of manipulation in that household."

Getting around men and manipulating them has been the usual way for women to develop alliances. As we saw in Chapter IV, Ann is trying to encourage her own daughter to be more straightforward. She described to me the process by which she herself has been learning to be less manipulative toward her husband, a change that relates directly to her sense of herself as an independent person with her own career.

"Mother will avoid conflict; that's where I learned it. We did a lot of keeping Daddy in good humor, quite openly. I remember her saying, 'Why don't you go in and see if you can get him into a good mood before dinner, because we have to tell him such-and-such.' I knew that, given something she really wanted, she would have her way, and probably gracefully, perhaps without his knowing it had ever happened. At the same time, she didn't want to cross him or be in conflict with him.

"I would find myself dealing with my husband that way. It's only been in the past five years that I've been able to be more direct, and I still have to stop and think. He's not used to being manipulated; he does everything straight on. It was so much easier for me to manipulate him than to meet him head-on, which was something I had no experience in. Even now, when I'm making my own money, I have to take myself in hand and say, 'Okay, I needed a new pair of shoes, I can put it right there on the check stub, even though they were too expensive.' Of course, he wouldn't say anything anyway, but it's hard for me to realize that I don't have to hide it, or manipulate it somehow. And the thing is, manipulation is unfair to him; it's a denial of his compassion and dignity. You're saying that he can't deal with the fact that you spent $12 too much for a pair of shoes.

"I know now when mother is trying to manipulate me, and I will just short-circuit the whole thing and get right at it. She hardly does it any more, though. Sometimes I will see her manipulating the children; I try not to get mixed up with it because I think they've got to learn how to deal with it."

Women do continue to get married at a great rate, even though they can see that many older women are dissatisfied with the options they have taken. I talked to Olivia Halstead just three weeks before her marriage. She is twenty-seven, still a relatively late age to marry. She had worked for several years after college, and has known her fiancé for two years. She plans to go on working after her marriage, and doesn't want to have any children.

"Right after I finished college, my mother would describe my life as just transitory until I got married. Real life for her was being married and having babies. What I was doing—working, living in the city—was a game, not real. That really burned me up. There I was going through the agonies of life, handling New York and an affair, and she was saying it wasn't real. But she's not overjoyed at all about my getting married; she's not saying this is her shining moment, she's finally succeeded. She's being very reasonable about the wedding plans, although for the most part she's getting her way.

"I'm not entirely sure what my marriage means to my mother. I thought she'd be relieved. Maybe if I'd done it when I was younger she would have had a stronger reaction. But maybe because I've been living alone, and proved I can get along by myself, she's less excited about it. Maybe she thinks marriage isn't *the* answer, so for that reason it might not work out. She likes my fiancé, but she's not mad about him. She doesn't know him very well. But I think it's the nature of the beast that she won't be mad about him. Maybe she thinks I'm giving up a good thing for a less good thing, which comes as a surprise, although she's never said anything. She began working three years ago; since then she's never said anything about my getting married. Since she's been working she's been questioning everything. It's really expanded her horizons. I know she was worried that she had been so overbearing and that the family background had been so unhappy that I would be very unhappy sexually. She has asked me some leading questions about that, but I have just not responded. Part of my real fear is that my parents didn't get along very well; they had a horrible marriage, really, but they stuck together because they wanted to.

"Marriage is really like satisfying a tribal ritual. I feel that in getting married I'm doing what's expected of me. Men get married because they think it will be good for them; women get married because they think it's a good thing."

VIII

FREE WOMEN

After the period of rivalry and conflict in adolescence, daughters are still largely expected to "settle down" and accept a role like their mothers'—to become like their mothers and therefore both an extension of them and a vindication of their lives. As the discontinuities in the lives of women have become more pronounced, however, more and more young women are reacting to the double message by choosing to remain single and pursue some serious work rather than immediately fall into the pattern of marriage and motherhood. Many of these young women may eventually marry, but when they do it will probably be for reasons different from their mothers'. They may marry for companionship or because they want to have children, but they are less likely to marry simply because it is expected of them or because they are established in a pattern of dependency. Some have decided against marriage altogether.

When daughters become adults and move out into the world on their own, the separation between mothers and daughters becomes a physical, if not immediately an emotional, reality. In fact, physical separation is often undertaken in the hope that emotional separation will follow. Both mothers and daughters have to adjust to a shift in the relationship when a daughter declares her independence from daughterhood without at the same time following her mother into a role as wife and, eventually, mother. Most often the daughter precipitates this separation, as Betty Gordon did when she moved out, but occasionally mothers themselves provide the push.

Among many women I interviewed, there occurred a moment of open confrontation between mother and daughter that marked the point at which their relationship changed, a moment when either a daughter or a mother declared her independence as a separate person, entitled to her own life space, and able to assume responsibility for herself. In doing this, a daughter is asserting her status as her mother's equal. But this equality is not the same as the equality she would have attained had she chosen the traditional route of motherhood. For a mother, such a moment is a declaration of independence from motherhood, and from responsibility for the continued dependency of her daughter.

Previous generations of daughters may have confronted their mothers over such issues as their choice of husbands. The daughters we are discussing in this chapter are involved in a different kind of confrontation—one based on a daughter's sense of herself, one that concerns only herself and her mother.

A confrontation is likely to occur if a daughter has already worked out her various dependency conflicts and has begun internally to define her own life space, her own sense of self over and against her mother's. A confrontation, then, openly establishes a daughter's new sense of herself, and it is up to her mother to decide whether to accept a new relationship based on greater equality. This is different from ongoing conflicts, which are often covert and bitter, and do not necessarily end in separation.

For many young women, going away to college represents the first big break with their mothers, and their own first real confrontation with the double message. Meg Hampton is a twenty-six-year-old medical student. She was born and raised in Alabama, in a small town where her grandfather ran the family business. Her mother had gone to college, where "she had the best time she ever had in her life." But when Meg's mother went to Mobile to get a job after graduating, it was too much for her parents, who pressured her into coming home and marrying a man they had picked out for her, who was slated to take over the family business someday. Meg recalls growing up with the double message very clearly expressed: "My mother wanted my sister and me to be the smartest kids in town; she got us books, and encouraged us. She also wanted us to get out of Alabama and go to college, preferably her college.

"At the same time, I was supposed to be pretty and popular, which I never was. My mother was attractive, but she never quite believed it, and she would spend a lot of money on clothes, hair, and makeup; I remember her once coming back from a shopping trip and saying she had spent $50 on makeup.

"The other thing was that she could never bear to have me leave home; we used to have terrible fights whenever I went away to camp. She would never quite bring herself to say she didn't want me to go, so instead she would criticize the clothes I wanted to take, and I would wind up in tears, and then she would tell me I was too immature to go away by myself. I was supposed to achieve, but at the same time she didn't think I could do anything.

"As soon as I did go away to college I stopped getting along with her; I think she didn't like the fact that I had gotten out from under her control. We fought every time I came home. She was always particularly critical of my choice of friends. Now I realize that she had nothing but her children, and she didn't want anybody coming between her and us. Yet she was pushing me very hard to get married until quite recently.

"In college I was never sure whether I wanted to be a serious student or someone who played around and went to parties a lot, and I switched around from semester to semester. Being smart and being pretty seemed to be mutually exclusive."

Lydia Jessel is twenty-three, and plans not to get married. She was brought up in Iowa, where her parents and married sister still live. Next fall she will go to business school. "When I went away to college, I insulted my mother. She didn't want me going away from home. I think she knew she had tremendous influence over me emotionally, and tremendous control over me, and that I was trying to get away from that. She and my father are very conservative Republicans, and also very religious; at college I became an atheist and a radical. My mother thought I was being duped by radicals; she always relied on religion and the Republican party to tell her what to do, so in her terms I could only be duped. She didn't believe it was possible for me to think things out for myself; that idea was very threatening to her.

"In high school we fought over relationships with boys; in college we fought over politics, religion, and the Vietnam war. Mother took my rejection of religion very personally; she thought it meant I was rejecting the essence of her morality. She wondered what kind of person I would be without a belief in the Christian ethic. She really took it so personally that she made me feel guilty for rejecting her. I would tell her I had a basic belief in ethics that did come from her, but that wasn't enough for her. It was as if she were saying that because what she had given me came from religion, by rejecting religion I was rejecting her."

Betty Gordon, whose mother we met in Chapter VI, also plans not to get married. She went to Boston after she dropped out of college. Now, at the age of twenty-two she is putting herself through school. "My mother always pushed me to go to college, but not in order to have a career. It was because she thought I needed an education to get a good husband, and I would get more respect from a husband if he knew I could get a job if I had to. Not that I should have to;

it was much better to get married and have a husband who made a lot of money. I thought that was a silly reason for going to college.

"I think she was very negative about what it was possible for a woman to do. She would say girls didn't go to medical school, but if I wanted to work I might think about medical technology. It was assumed that what I really wanted to do, and would do, was get married."

Three different daughters, whose mothers in different ways gave them the same message. Meg's dilemma in college is not an unusual one for bright, serious girls who have been raised on the double message by mothers who were not themselves secure in their own sense of femininity. This is one of the great paradoxes of the double message: the emphasis on superficial qualities of "femininity" helps create an insecure sense of self-worth in women who hope that their daughters will become the attractive beauties they never felt themselves to be. And they pass on to their daughters their own sense of insecurity about their femininity. Then, having given in to the dependency side of the double message, they encourage their daughters to achieve and at the same time disparage their ability to do so. Their insecurity about both possibilities is passed on to their daughters.

Lydia's mother took her intellectual defection so personally that Lydia felt guilty; her intellectual independence was interpreted by her mother as a personal attack. Lydia sees that her own new attitudes were in fact part of her struggle to get out from under her mother's control, so to some extent her mother's interpretation was correct. Just as in early childhood, a mother's attitude toward her daughter's increasing independence can have an important effect on the way a daughter perceives herself. Lydia had a difficult choice: to continue on her own path and deal with her guilt in her own way, or to give in to her mother's values and feel, by extension, that whenever she took a strong stand she would be doing a personal injury to someone else.

For Betty, the message was in simpler terms: achievement

meant getting a good husband. Not surprisingly, Betty received this as a message telling her there was really not much point in going to college at all.

In Chapter IV we saw how, as early as junior high school, daughters are beginning to recognize that academic success will complicate their lives as women. By the time they get to college, many women begin, almost deliberately it would seem, to "fail" intellectually.[1] Matina Horner, a psychologist who is now president of Radcliffe College, has documented this phenomenon in a number of articles. She shows that bright college women, when pitted against men in experimental situations, will feel they must fail in order to preserve not merely their social standing but really their very lives. In tests asking for responses to a hypothetical situation in which a woman was head of her class in medical school, women tended to predict either that something horrible happened to her or that she quickly realized the gravity of her situation and stopped trying for top marks. Another reaction was that she wasn't a real woman at all; she had been made up by a group of men.

If one considers the messages Lydia, Meg, and Betty received from their mothers, such responses make sense. If you can't integrate achievement and femininity, if you are made to feel that competitiveness is a personal threat, or if your achievement simply is not valued, it will seem easier to fail. If you think your competitiveness will hurt someone else, as Lydia's mother implied to her, you are likely by projection to fear that someone will hurt *you*.

But there were elements in the lives of these three young women that made a difference. One was changing times. In earlier days a daughter might run off and get married to 'get out from under' her mother. It is now accepted, at least in middle-class families, that daughters may go off to work on their own after college, or even in lieu of college. But by and large this is still considered to be an interim period before a daughter gets married and settles down, or in which she expands her chances of finding a suitable husband. Daughters who see such a migration as a stepping-stone to their own future careers remain in the minority, although their numbers are growing.

All three daughters were in conflict with their mothers. Meg and Lydia seem to have kept up an open argument with their mothers. They were pushing for their freedom and testing their mothers' responses even while absorbing the double message. Betty seems to have been quieter about it, but she clearly had her own opinion.

Finally, all three seem to have found sources of strength in their mothers, no matter how confused the messages about achievement were. Meg says of her mother, "She is a very talented businesswoman, but felt she should get married, so she never had room to use her talent. It never occurred to her to work, because she didn't have to. Other women in the family had worked because they had to, for economic reasons: my grandmother worked in the business until it became successful, and one of my aunts is a teacher. Recognizing my mother's abilities has helped me see how I got where I am. There was something in her that made her push us more than other girls were pushed by their mothers, and I appreciate that. I guess I hold onto it as something my mother did for me that was good; it balances out the things she did that I think were destructive, like passing on social pressures."

Lydia recalled, "My mother thrived on having children, and when my sister and I were little we all did a lot of things together. I always felt that in some ways she was much stronger than my father; I find it hard to believe that if she really wanted to do something she wouldn't do it."

Betty says, "I probably use my mother as a model, unconsciously. I respect her for the fact that she raised five kids, which wasn't easy, and managed to keep on top of the situation. I see her as a tragic kind of figure because she doesn't seem to have fulfilled herself completely as a woman, and she depended so much on family for her identity. I'm not sure what I get from her specifically, but I admire it."

All three left home to pursue their own interests. Meg at first had no idea of going to medical school: "I can't imagine not working; that's been clear to me since I went to college. But I had no idea what I wanted to do, so I came to New York and got a job teaching in a private school. My mother didn't mind that; it was a socially acceptable alternative to getting married."

But Meg's independence included a new life style and new interests that finally led to a confrontation with her mother: "Three years ago she came to see me, and we had a hard time of it. Her conception of New York is high-rise apartments, theater, and fancy restaurants. I was living in a tenement on the Lower East Side and working in a neighborhood health clinic in my spare time. She was horrified. She came on Saturday; on Sunday we had a twelve-hour fight that started at breakfast when she announced that she was going to church and expected me to come with her. I said no, and she got very upset because I didn't believe in God anymore. Then she switched to something else because she doesn't like to deal with big issues; she'd rather fight over trivia.

"After she came back from church she announced she was leaving immediately. We fought until eleven or twelve that night. She said I belonged to her; I was her child. I told her I didn't belong to her. She said she had always tried to do the best for me and now I wasn't doing what she wanted; she didn't like the way I was living, and it reflected badly on her. I wasn't going to give an inch. I felt that if I said 'you're right' just once she would suck me in, and I would cease being my own person.

"At one point she packed her bags and started to walk out of the apartment. I did ask her to come back then; I decided there was no point in totally breaking off communications, which is what would have happened; she would have felt I had kicked her out. So she stayed, and for the rest of the week we got along very civilly; by the time she left we were on good terms. That was definitely a personal victory for me; it was a turning point in many ways.

"I had begun thinking about medical school, and I think that argument with my mother was part of the process of realizing that I wanted to do something of my own, something that would mean I was really taking myself seriously. That fight somehow broke some of my old ties and conflicts. Lately I've been thinking of myself as an attractive person who can have relationships with men on my own terms; I guess I've begun to resolve that conflict in myself between achieving and being pretty.

"My mother has also begun to respect me. She used to sit at the dinner table saying, 'Your hair looks terrible, your table manners are terrible,' until I crumbled, and she would turn on me and say, 'I had no idea you were so immature.' But the last time I was home we got along beautifully. I felt much less defensive, and we were both able to compromise. I let her take me shopping, which she loves, but I made her buy me blue jeans, which is what I wear most of the time."

Meg has found that her mother is able to stand on her own very well, and that this separation has enabled them both to grow as persons. "Recently I have the feeling that she is starting to think more about what she can do for herself. She has been taking finance courses, and is really running the business now. She went to work there after my father died, but I think her ideal was always to be taken care of by one of us. But my sister has left also. So I think my mother has begun to feel less helpless. And I've been telling her that there are lots of advantages to having a doctor in the family."

Because mother–daughter relationships are virtually confined to an emotional, personal sphere, confrontations between them tend to be emotionally stormy, in a way that scenes between fathers and sons usually are not.

Lydia recalls, "When I came to New York, I insulted my mother again. She saw it as the final rejection, and it made her angry. When I was growing up she used to tell us constantly that she was doing everything for us and that her whole life was miserable because of us. After I got my own apartment she began calling me to complain about her life, or about my father, and it made me nervous.

"Then, the last time I was home, she put on a real show; I thought she was going to have a heart attack. For two days she was furious with my father, and with me because I didn't get up early to help her out. She would run up and down the stairs and yell at one or the other of us. Finally she and I really had it out, in a screaming, crying fight. And when we had calmed down, I think we had achieved a new understanding. I confronted her with the fact that she was doing this to make me feel she had given up everything and ruined her life to take care of us. I told her, 'This isn't necessary. I think I appreciate what you've done, but you're going to have a heart attack if you keep this up.' And she dealt with it; she has never been quite as hysterical since. I'm convinced that she doesn't carry on like this when I'm not there. And basically, I don't think she really does feel all that sorry about her life."

Betty's story is a little different: she couldn't see any point to staying in college, so she dropped out. "When I came to Boston, my mother really didn't think I could survive. She thought I would never get a job, and that I would wind up in trouble. But I got a secretarial job, and after a while I began to hate it. I felt very lazy. I kept saying, 'Look at all these people who work hard and get promoted, and I don't care.' I was really rationalizing. I had hated the way my father worked hard, and put so much value in working so there would be money, but never had time to be home.

"Then I decided to go back to college; I'm still working, and putting myself through, and now my mother kind of admires the fact that I'm doing it. I don't think she really believed that I would. She still has conflicts about it; I think she would rather I was back home or married. But we get along pretty well now."

Marjorie Gordon herself feels that she has completely accepted Betty's choice. (Like most people, mothers and daughters seldom have quite the same view of any situation in which they are both involved.) "Up until a short time ago I would have said that there was a big difference between my relationship with Betty and my relationships with my married daughters. Betty was pioneering, fighting for personal freedom of a kind the others never seemed to want as much. But I think that what has made a difference with Betty is that she has proved she is responsible; she has done what she set out to do. She kept a job, and she has begun to take college courses. She's begun to realize that she wasn't really prepared for anything, and I think she sees that we wanted her to take the time to prepare herself.

"Now, I would say I have a similar relationship with all my daughters. We are friends, and we can talk about anything. Betty has been away long enough, she is experienced enough, she has a head on her shoulders and she really knows what she is doing. We have had to learn to respect her choice of life, and accept it, and she feels more secure about her own choice now."

A freeing confrontation can happen between a married daughter and her mother, also. As with single women, it is a confrontation involving the two women directly, husbands have no part in it. Grace Raphaelson, whom we met in Chapter V, found herself having such a confrontation with her mother as she became more assertive about her own life.

"My mother always visited us quite often; she is widowed now, and she tends to spend as much time as she can with each of her children. I can understand that, but at one point it became too much for me. She had come into town for a bridge tournament and she was just staying too long. We don't have an extra bedroom, and I had to double up with my daughter. Finally I told my mother, 'My daughter has had to give up her room for two weeks now, and it's disruptive. I'd appreciate it if you'd make arrangements to leave right after the tournament.' She got very excited, almost hysterical, and in five minutes had packed her bag, come downstairs with her airline ticket, and said she was leaving immediately. Well, the upshot was that she didn't, she stayed a few days more. But I really felt that I had in a sense unstuck my mother. I said, 'I'm a person, understand my sensitivity right now, and you'll have to make other arrangements.' I don't know what will happen to our relationship; we still have one, but it's bound to be different. One thing leads to another; I've got my head together and I feel ready to conquer the world. I'm unsticking myself. The funny thing is that I see now that as I'm unsticking my mother I'm also beginning to unstick my daughter. I find I just don't have the time to oversee her every minute anymore, and she's learning to take more responsibility."

The traditions, then, are changing; more daughters are establishing themselves as their own women, proving to themselves that they can be self-supporting and independent. Traditional mothers, themselves raised with the idea that a daughter goes from dependence on her parents to dependence on her husband, naturally feel doubtful about a daughter's ability to make it on her own. Yet, whether through conflict and confrontation or sheer perseverence, or both, daughters are demonstrating their ability to find their own way. In doing so they are playing a role for which they have no direct model. And so, really, are their mothers. Both mothers and daughters may express their ambivalence in a variety of ways; the extraordinary thing is how they are adapting themselves and communicating their changing concepts of themselves to each other.

Feminism has helped create a climate of support for young women who want to change their roles. But it isn't always daughters who are doing the separating. More and more older mothers are finding, as Marjorie Gordon did with Julie, her youngest daughter, that they are ready to give up mothering their grown daughters before their daughters are ready to break their own dependency. Alice Litvinak found herself having to initiate a confrontation that pushed her and her daughter into psychic independence. "I had always wanted a daughter; I had a lot of fantasies about dressing her in pretty clothes and so forth. My mother had had her own strong fantasies about me, in all of which I disappointed her. But what did not exist in reality she fantasized; she made me, in her own mind, something that I was not. I would have loved to fulfill her fantasies of my being a beautiful, romantic young woman, but I couldn't. I became a serious student and went on to graduate school. In a sense I didn't really rebel; I just couldn't be what my mother wanted me to be. I think a lot of young women have rebelled because they felt they wanted to be themselves; I rebelled by default.

"I'm surprised now to realize that I did the same thing to my daughter that my mother did to me, except I think I was more subtle than my mother was. But at first my daughter was able to fulfill that role in reality. She was very pretty and very sweet until she became an adolescent. Then she had the same weight problem I had had, and she didn't feel attractive to boys. She wasn't what I wanted her to be, and perhaps not what she wanted to be. Yet I liked her as a person all the time.

"I had always worked, and had urged her to plan a career for herself. It was the same old double message: be beautiful, sexy, and attractive and also be strong, make a lot of money, and control your own destiny. It's an impossible job, I realize now. But it came to me as a shock when she graduated from college and became very frightened about what she was going to do with her life. She wanted to get married, so I set myself out to help her. She dieted, and we went on spending sprees, and had her hair done. I was right there behind her, helping her work toward a completely stereotyped role. I saw that she was picking up on the dependent, feminine side of the double message, but I decided that there was nothing I could do about it, that she would have to find her own way in her own time. I began to feel more

and more that I had very little control over what she was;
maybe she wasn't exactly what I wanted her to be, but I
liked her.

"Her anger came as a complete surprise. She felt she
wasn't getting where she wanted to go, and my reaction was
to be there whenever she needed me. The result was that we
began to have some really terrible scenes. She was living in
an apartment with friends, but she would come to see me
and suddenly tell me she was furious with me, at the same
time expecting me to take care of her as though she were
much younger—to do her laundry, for instance.

"Finally I told her that I didn't think she had a right to
behave this way or to keep raging at me without saying
specifically what I had done wrong. I couldn't accept the
idea that I should now be punished for being her mother. I
felt that she was old enough for me not to have to deal with
her emotional problems any more; I wanted to abdicate
from motherhood, and relate to her as an adult and as a
friend.

"We had an enormous fight; I told her I didn't think she
was treating me as a person but as some kind of stereotyped
mother. I told her I simply couldn't be a mother to her anymore; we were both too old. If we couldn't relate to each
other as friends, forget it. She couldn't handle that; she
couldn't give me up. I was more ready to give her up than
she was to give me up. And the trouble was that I knew she
didn't really hate me; she loved me and hated me both. But I
felt that unless I handled it head-on and asserted myself as a
person, we never would resolve this intense relationship.

"I didn't like the way she was living; she wasn't really
doing anything, just living with a group of friends in a big
house in Cambridge, doing odd jobs, and the women were
cooking. But I decided I would stay out of it altogether; it
seemed that the more I tried to talk to her the more antag-
onism was created.

"Now, the most amazing thing has happened. She has gotten her own apartment in Boston, she is working in a mental-

health clinic during the day and taking graduate courses in psychology at night. She wants to become a clinical psychologist. She is suddenly letting herself face a real challenge, and she is frightened, but she is finding out that other people are facing the same kinds of problems. And I am keeping hands off. If she wants to communicate with me, fine, but I'm leaving it up to her. Other mothers have told me they find my attitude unmotherly, even inhuman. It tears me apart, but I know she's got to struggle through by herself; more than anything else, I want her to be a strong woman."

As in adolescence, after rejection and conflict a process of internal reconciliation to reality occurs in both mother and daughter. This may or may not lead to external reconciliation, which depends a lot on the temperament and history of both mother and daughter. But when a real letting go has occurred, the other person, whether mother or daughter, is not lost. On both sides there is a reassessment of the relationship, and of one's own identity in relation to the other.

Alice Litvinak reflected on her view as a mother: "I would like my daughter to be a friend, a person with whom I can have an equal relationship, but I don't know whether that's possible between mothers and daughters. The only mothers and daughters I have seen get along well are those who are both absorbed in shopping, cooking, and raising children; then the mother becomes the grandmother and helps take care of the children, and sometimes it works out. But if they're both strong women, it's difficult. My feeling is that if mothers and daughters can't get along they ought to separate and go their own ways. This feeling that mothers and daughters have to love each other and feel guilty about each other is very detrimental. A son can move away from his mother but a daughter can't; she and her mother have to straighten it out; they have to love each other because a female's identity is more tied up with family relationships; she has to go on to become a mother and a wife. A son may have to go on to become a husband and father, but he has the escape valve of work. If a daughter doesn't make it in the family there is no place for her to make it.

"I don't know what my relationship with my daughter will turn into; there's no conclusion to this story. But I've learned that mothers don't have as much control over their daughters as they would like to think, and as they are told to have. And that's a relief. I've learned that all I can really do is to set an example and be my own person, and then she must choose whatever she wants to be. What it comes down to is that I owe myself more than I owe her; in doing more for myself I think I'm doing more for her. I think we would be doing a service to our daughters by not acting like everything is our fault; then maybe all of us will deal more with the world, rather than blaming each other and ourselves when things go wrong."

Meg Hampton expressed a daughter's opinion: "I'm not terribly hopeful about being able to relate well to my mother, although I'd like to be on good terms with her, as long as they're my terms.

"I see a lot of my mother in myself, and I fight it sometimes. I find myself choosing the colors she likes, and judging people by her terms. I carry her around in my head, and sometimes I know I'm looking at things through her eyes. When I first came to New York, I would find myself becoming friendly with people I knew she wouldn't like, and thinking, 'I couldn't take this person home.' Although I couldn't anyway—it's too far. But I'm slowly becoming aware of which are her judgments and which are mine, at the same time recognizing that I'm her daughter, and I can't change that. I think that by moving so far away from home and doing something so different from what she expected, I've been trying to pull myself up by the roots and make myself over into a new person. But I've come to realize that's not really possible or even desirable. Instead, what I can do is to bring the past in and let it be there, but in constructive ways. It's all right to like the same colors my mother likes, but I don't need to judge my friends on her terms."

"Maybe you're accepting your mother the way she really is, and saying 'Okay, I'm a different person,' and working from there," I said.

With Meg Hampton, Alice Litvinak, and the other women in this chapter, we have come full circle. The young mothers in earlier chapters are trying to help their daughters achieve the kind of separation that Meg has only begun to earn for herself in adulthood and that Alice has helped her adult daughter find by refusing, finally, to continue to support her in dependency. With all the mothers and daughters in this book, the point of separation, at whatever age, has been the point at which they come to recognize themselves, and so each other, as separate people. In most cases this recognition seems to have come when a daughter realized that her identity did not have to be bound up completely in her mother's identity and role, or when a mother separated herself from her own role as mother of her daughter.

For small daughters, the point of separation from their mothers traditionally has been seen as the point at which they turned toward their fathers, and, indeed, this is one aspect of separating. But, as we have seen, when mothers have little sense of their own identity, the turn toward men can be merely a mask behind which an intense mother–daughter relationship continues unabated. And in adolescence and adulthood, relationships with men can be used by both mothers and daughters as means of continuing their conflict.

Becoming a mother in her own right is also considered to be a time of growth and separation from one's mother, and this is often the case. But if a daughter merely assumes her mother's role, she does not achieve a real sense of herself as an individual who can support her own daughter's separation into selfhood.

Real connection with the outside world through work seems to have been an important element in many women's finding themselves as separate people, but if they feel too conflicted about their new role, they may not be able to integrate it with other aspects of their identity. Work, too, can provide a mask for a continuing overinvolvement between mothers and daughters.

There are different kinds of separation at different stages of life. Most of the daughters in this book have received enough support from their mothers to emerge from the stage of complete symbiosis in early infancy. But for the vast majority of mothers and daughters, this emergence remains only partial. At some level mothers and daughters tend to remain emotionally bound up with each other in what might be called a semisymbiotic relationship, in which neither ever quite sees herself or the other as a separate person. Roles have played an important part in keeping this circle going. Role identity has become increasingly narrowly defined and overemphasized in a society that has been bent on ever greater specialization. Women's roles, as they have evolved in our society, work against the development of a secure sense of personal and sexual identity and, conversely, these insecurities feed into a reliance on roles for self-definition. But roles alone are not the whole story; neither getting married, nor having a baby, nor work can, by itself, create or destroy a sense of self.

What matters is how women view themselves and their activities in society. This personal vision is conditioned by the way society views women, but we are not only creatures of our social training. Women themselves have been working for generations to push back the boundaries of their roles to make room for themselves in the world. Mothers who have passed along a double message to their daughters have been part of this slow awakening, and mothers who have somehow managed to find a secure sense of themselves have been able to support their daughters in behavior that goes beyond roles.

Young mothers today are beginning to think about how to help their daughters become strong people. They are revising their sense of themselves in relation to men, to their own

mothers, and to the world. It may be that women are beginning to break the lock that the whole concept of roles has
placed on our thinking about ourselves. Finally, neither
what you do nor who you are is a role. What you think you
can do, what you do, and how you do it will reflect and help
determine your sense of yourself. The world and the self
interact to make us who we think we are. As mothers and
daughters begin to change their ways of thinking about
themselves and each other, they are changing society.

NOTES

INTRODUCTION

1. Erik H. Erikson, *Identity: Youth and Crisis* (New York: Norton, 1968), p. 283. In this book and in his better-known *Childhood and Society*, Erikson elaborates his conception of woman's identity in terms of an inner space that must be integrated into the sense of self.
2. The woman who did not want to be a person was quoted in *The New York Times*, February 7, 1975.
3. See Nancy Chodorow, "Family Structure and Feminine Personality," in *Women, Culture and Society*, edited by Michelle Simbalist Rosaldo and Louise Lamphere (Stanford, Calif.: Stanford University Press, 1974), pp. 43–66. This essay refers to work in a number of different disciplines to establish the thesis that women in our society are forced to remain infantile and so have a stake in keeping their daughters infantile. It is a landmark essay, and the anthology in which it is contained offers some of the most important writing on women to be found anywhere.
4. Clara Thompson, "Cultural Pressures on the Psychology of Women," in *Interpersonal Relationships: The Selected Papers of Clara M. Thompson*, edited by Maurice R. Green (New York: Basic Books, 1964), p. 240. (Originally published in *Psychiatry*, 5 (1942): 331–339.) Clara Thompson and Karen Horney were the first major psy-

choanalytic investigators to offer coherent theories of feminine development in opposition to many of Freud's ideas. Both are extremely readable, and both anticipated by many years much of the thinking of modern feminists.

CHAPTER I

1. See Grete L. Bibring, M.D., "Some Considerations of the Psychological Processes in Pregnancy," in *The Psychoanalytic Study of the Child*, vol. 14 (New York: International Universities Press, 1959); G. L. Bibring, T. F. Dwyer, D. S. Huntington, and A. F. Valenstein, "A Study of the Earliest Mother–Child Relationship: I. Some Propositions and Comments," in *The Psychoanalytic Study of the Child*, vol. 16 (New York: International Universities Press, 1961). The work of Dr. Bibring and her colleagues represents a departure in thinking about pregnancy and birth as a normal developmental period in which psychological symptoms are not necessarily evidence of deep-lying neuroses but can be related very directly to the new mother's immediate tasks of adjustment. A related essay by Dr. Bibring appears in Signe Hammer, *Women: Body and Culture* (New York: Harper & Row, 1975).

2. See Niles Newton, "Trebly Sensuous Woman," *Psychology Today* (July 1971): 68–71, 98–99. Dr. Newton has worked for many years in the psychology of child bearing.

3. Helene Deutsch, *The Psychology of Women*, vol. 2 (New York: Grune & Stratton, 1945), p. 213. Dr. Deutsch's two-volume study remains the most extensive application of Freudian theory to the study of feminine development. For this reason it is often dismissed as outdated. But despite an emphasis on the active–passive dichotomy and on masochism as a factor in feminine development, Dr. Deutsch offers much useful case material and many valid insights.

4. The Psychoanalyst Margaret Mahler has evolved the theory of the separation–individuation process, in which the in-

fant arrives at a sense of itself as an individual through a gradual process of separation from the mother. Mahler's work is an important contribution to ego psychology, a modern development in psychoanalysis dealing with the development of the ego, or sense of self, as much more than a mediator between the id and the superego. In studying her theory, I consulted the following essays: "Thoughts About Development and Individuation," *The Psychoanalytic Study of the Child*, vol. 18 (1963), pp. 307–324; "On the Significance of the Normal Separation–Individuation Phase," *Drives, Affects, Behavior*, vol. 2 (1965), pp. 161–169; "On Human Symbiosis and the Vicissitudes of Individuation," *Journal of the American Psychoanalytic Association*, 15:4 (1967): 740–762; "A Study of the Separation–Individuation Process," *The Psychoanalytic Study of the Child*, vol. 26 (1971), pp. 403–424.

5. One major exception is the psychoanalyst Edith Jacobson, whose *The Self and the Object World* (New York: International Universities Press, 1964), deals extensively with the personality development of girls in relation to their mothers. This is a difficult but valuable contribution to ego psychology.

6. Dr. Marjorie Taggart White, personal communication 1975.

7. Chodorow, *op. cit.*

8. See David Gutmann, "Women and the Conception of Ego Strength," *Merrill-Palmer Quarterly of Behavior and Development* 11:3 (1965): 229–240. Gutmann's theory that the structure of women's egos differs significantly from that of men is nicely rebutted in Nancy Chodorow's essay. Whatever the validity of Gutmann's thesis, he offers a clear statement of a widely held idea, or myth.

9. See Howard A. Moss, "Sex, Age, and State as Determinants of Mother–Infant Interaction," *Merrill-Palmer Quarterly of Behavior and Development* 13:1 (1967): 19–36; Michael Lewis, "There's No Unisex in the Nursery," *Psychology Today* (May 1972): 54–57.

10. The concept of "enabling" was suggested to me by Dr. Marjorie Taggart White.

CHAPTER II

1. See Margaret Mead, *Male and Female* (New York: Morrow, 1949), a classic investigation of the interplay between body and environment in the personality development of children in a variety of cultures, including our own. Her ideas, as expressed in this and other books, form part of the general background of my own thinking.

2. Erik H. Erikson, *Childhood and Society* (New York): Norton, 1950, 1963). This book contains Erikson's major theoretical formulations of the stages of identity and the idea of inner space.

3. See David B. Lynn, *Parental and Sex-Role Identification: A Theoretical Formulation* (Berkeley, Calif.: McCutchen, 1969), a fascinating book in which Lynn develops a series of hypotheses showing how boys and girls learn gender roles. Particularly interesting is his suggestion that boys must figure out their roles because they don't see much of their fathers, whereas girls identify more concretely and personally with their mothers. This is why boys grow up to be better at problem solving and abstract thinking than girls. On the other hand, girls whose mothers are distant tend also to develop skills in abstract thinking, and boys who have a close personal relationship with their fathers, as Eskimo boys do, are not better at problem solving than girls.

4. See Jerome Kagan and Howard A. Moss, *Birth to Maturity: A Study in Psychological Development* (New York: Wiley, 1962). A group of middle-class children and their parents were studied and analyzed as the children grew from infancy to adulthood.

5. See Lois Wladis Hoffman, "Early Childhood Experiences and Women's Achievement Motives," *Journal of Social Issues*, 28:2 (1972): 129–155. This is an invaluable survey of research into the ways girls are socialized to be dependent. This paper also is included in Signe Hammer, *Women: Body and Culture* (New York: Harper & Row, 1975.)

6. See Chodorow, *op. cit.*

7. See Erikson, *Childhood and Society*.

8. See Betty Friedan, *The Feminine Mystique* (New York: Norton, 1963; Dell paperback, 1964). Friedan was the first modern feminist to write about the ways women are infantilized by the conventions of femininity and to discuss women's needs to grow as persons. Also see Phillip Wylie, *Generation of Vipers* (New York: Rinehart, 1955. Wylie seems to have invented the terms "Mom" and "Momism," in writing about a son's view of the engulfing mother.

9. See John Money, *Man & Woman, Boy & Girl* (Baltimore: Johns Hopkins Press, 1972), an important book exploring the relationships between innate factors, such as hormones and genes, and social training in the determination of identity.

10. Mahler, *op. cit.*

11. Hoffman, *op. cit.*

12. See Bettye Caldwell et al., "Infant Day Care and Attachment," *American Journal of Orthopsychiatry*, 30 (1970): 397–412.

13. See H. Schaffer and P. Emerson, "The Development of Social Attachments in Infancy," *Monographs of the Society for Research in Child Development*, 20:3, Serial #94, 1964.

14. See Sarane Spence Boocock, "A Crosscultural Analysis of the Childcare System," prepared for the Russell Sage Foundation, 1974.

15. The example of the woman construction engineer was cited in *The New York Times*, April 29, 1974.

CHAPTER III

1. Mahler, *op. cit.*

2. Erikson, *Childhood and Society*.

3. Erikson, *Ibid.*, p. 64. (The idea that girls are particularly sensitive to invasions is my own.)

4. See Alfred C. Kinsey, Wardell B. Pomeroy, Clyde E. Martin, and Paul H. Gebhard, *Sexual Behavior in the Human Female* (Philadelphia: Saunders, 1953).

5. In his essay, "The Transformations of Puberty" (in *Three*

Essays on the Theory of Sexuality, first published in 1905, republished by New York: Basic Books, 1962), Freud states that at puberty the sexuality of girls, which up to this point has been "masculine," is overcome by repression, and that only a woman "who holds herself back and who denies her sexuality" can arouse the sexuality of a man. In this curious equation, it seems clear that "feminine" development is considered to depend on the absence or denial of sexuality.

6. See Karen Horney's papers on female sexuality in *Feminine Psychology*, edited by Harold Kelman, M.D. (New York: Norton, 1967). Clara Thompson's selected papers were cited in the introduction; her papers on women also appear in a paperback, *On Women*, edited by Maurice R. Green (New York: New American Library, 1971). Also see William H. Masters and Virginia E. Johnson, *Human Sexual Response* (Boston: Little, Brown, 1966). This is a difficult but important book, which gives the results of extensive laboratory investigation of sexual response in men and women.

7. Sigmund Freud, "Female Sexuality," in *Collected Papers*, vol. 5 (London: Hogarth, 1950). Like much of Freud's work, this essay has been reprinted in many different collections.

8. Jacobson, *op. cit.*

9. In her essay "Changing Concepts of Homosexuality in Psychoanalysis," Clara Thompson suggests that "a very important determining influence in the development of homosexuality" may be parents' dissappointment in the child's sex, "especially if their disappointment leads them to treat the child as if he were of the opposite sex." One can assume that a mother who is comfortable with her own sexuality would not be likely to disapprove of her daughter's developing sexual identity.

10. Dr. Marjorie Taggart White, personal communication 1975.

11. Jacobson, *op. cit.*

12. Clara Thompson, "Cultural Pressures in the Psychology of Women," *On Women*, p. 137.

13. Money, *op. cit.*, p. 164.

14. Clara Thompson, "Some Effects of the Derogatory Attitude toward Female Sexuality," *On Women*, p. 149.
15. Jacobson, *op. cit.*

CHAPTER IV

1. Jacobson, *op. cit.*
2. Ann Oakley, *Housewife* (New York: Pantheon, 1974). This is a lucid, intelligent study of the effects of industrialization on the role of women, particularly in England, and an analysis of various modern myths about "woman's place." Oakley shows very clearly how industrialization has led to the opposition of home and work, with a resulting narrowing of the scope of women's activities in society.
3. Philippe Ariès, *Centuries of Childhood: A Social History of Family Life*, trans. from the French by Robert Baldick (New York: Vintage, 1962). This is a landmark study of the evolution of the idea of childhood and its relationship to the evolution of our modern concept of the family. Although Ariès focuses primarily on boys—the position of girls remained unchanged until quite recently —he offers devastating evidence that the development of the modern family depended on the "slow and steady deterioration of the wife's position in the household" (p. 356).
4. Elizabeth Janeway, *Man's World, Woman's Place, A Study in Social Mythology* (New York: Morrow, 1971). This perceptive study offers extensive discussion of the narrowed scope of women's activities in modern society, relating the loss of direct ties with the outside world to "the loss of an objective standard by which to measure oneself and one's actions" (p. 170). The greater subjectiveness of women, then, is seen as a consequence of their social role, rather than of any natural predilection.
5. Ariès, *op. cit.*
6. Fear of success has been investigated and documented in a number of essays by Matina Horner. A concise statement

of her work appears in "Fail: Bright Women," *Psychology Today*, November 1969, pp. 36, 38, 62.

7. See Margaret M. Hennig, "Family Dynamics for Developing Positive Achievement Motivation in Women: the Successful Woman Executive," in *Women & Success: The Anatomy of Achievement*, edited by Ruth B. Kundsin, Sc.D. (New York: Morrow, 1973). This is a useful collection of articles exploring the relationship between individual psychology, gender-role expectations, and other factors in the development of successfully achieving women.

CHAPTER V

1. See Natalie Shainess, "A Re-evaluation of Some Aspects of Femininity through a Study of Menstruation: A Preliminary Report," in *Science and Psychoanalysis*, vol. 5, edited by Jules H. Masserman, M.D. (New York: Grune & Stratton, 1962), pp. 278–285.

2. Horner, *op. cit.*

3. The search for an ideal mother is my own idea, growing out of the interview material. It is broadly based on psychoanalytic concepts of the ego ideal, discussions of which can be found, for example, in the works of Erik Erikson and Edith Jacobson.

4. Erik Erikson discusses his concept of the inner space in both *Childhood and Society* and *Identity: Youth and Crisis*. His concept is useful, but he carries it to extremes by suggesting that women's activities in the world should somehow relate to this biological configuration.

5. Ronald D. Laing, *The Politics of The Family* (New York: Pantheon, 1971). Laing's work is sufficiently well known to need no introduction; it is significant that much of his work has focused on the mystification of daughters' identities.

6. Anorexia is discussed in an article by Sam Blum, "Children Who Starve Themselves," *The New York Times Magazine*, 10 November 1974. A relationship between drug addiction and inadequate separation from the mother was

suggested to me by Joanne Turo, psychologist and co-ordinator of clinical services and director of treatment at Greenwich House Counseling Center, an outpatient therapy center for drug addicts.

CHAPTER VII

1. The psychoanalyst Ruth Moulton discusses some of the relationships among love, work, sexuality, and the mother–daughter relationship in "Multiple Factors in Frigidity," originally published in *Science and Psychoanalysis*, vol. X, edited by Jules H. Masserman, M.D. (New York: Grune & Stratton, 1968), pp. 75–93. This essay is also included in Hammer, *Women: Body and Culture*.
2. Freud, "Female Sexuality."

CHAPTER VIII

1. Horner, *op. cit.*